GLASGOW UNCOVERED

The Complete Walking Guide: Eighteen
Kelvingrove to the Cathedral, Ashton Lan

Veyla Fenwick

DISCLAIMER

This book is intended as an informative and interpretive guide to the cultural, historical, and social landscapes of Glasgow. While every effort has been made to ensure accuracy and clarity, the content is based on a combination of public information, historical records, personal accounts, interviews, research materials, and subjective interpretation. Readers should be aware that cities are living, changing entities. As such, some information—especially concerning venues, public artworks, community projects, and local businesses—may change over time.

The views expressed in this book are those of the author and contributors and do not necessarily reflect the official policies or positions of any institutions, organizations, or communities mentioned herein. This book aims to celebrate Glasgow in all its complexity, including its struggles and triumphs, and has been written with deep respect for the people and places represented. However, any errors or omissions are entirely unintentional.

This publication may refer to sensitive topics including urban poverty, migration, displacement, sectarianism, and political activism. These subjects are approached with care, but interpretations and memories vary. The inclusion of oral histories, local legends, and community narratives does not imply factual verification in every case; instead, these accounts are included to honor the lived experiences that shape the city's collective identity.

The author and publisher do not accept any liability for loss, injury, inconvenience, or damage sustained by any person using or relying on the information contained in this publication. Readers are encouraged to independently verify addresses, opening hours, and safety considerations, and to consult local sources where possible.

No part of this book is intended to infringe upon any existing rights. All trademarks, service marks, and copyrights used are the property of their respective owners and are used for identification purposes only.

If you believe any information in this book requires correction or further attribution, we welcome your feedback and will endeavor to respond respectfully and promptly.

TABLE OF CONTENTS

Introduction: Walking Glasgow – A City of Layers — 4

Chapter 1: The Beating Heart – City Centre and the Clyde — 7
- 1.1 Buchanan Street to George Square: Glasgow's Commercial Pulse — 16
- 1.2 Merchant City – From Tobacco Lords to Creative Quarters — 20
- 1.3 Sauchiehall Street and Garnethill: Culture, Nightlife, and Creativity — 26
- 1.4 Anderston and Argyle Street: Echoes of Industry and Innovation — 31
- 1.5 The Clyde Waterfront: Regeneration and Resilience — 37

Chapter 2: The Storied West – Wealth, Art, and Activism — 44
- 2.1 Kelvingrove and the University of Glasgow: Knowledge and Empire — 44
- 2.2 Ashton Lane and Byres Road: Bohemia and Boutique — 50
- 2.3 Hillhead and the Lanes: Literary Glasgow and Local Life — 55
- 2.4 Maryhill and the Forth & Clyde Canal: Working-Class Pride and Waterways — 60
- 2.5 Dowanhill and Hyndland: Garden Suburbs and Quiet Power — 65

Chapter 3: The East – Roots, Resistance, and Renewal — 71
- 3.1 High Street to Glasgow Cathedral: Origins of a City — 71
- 3.2 Dennistoun and Alexandra Parade: Tenements and Transformation — 76
- 3.3 The Barras, Calton, and Glasgow Green: Markets, Music, and Memory — 81
- 3.4 Duke Street to Parkhead: Football, Faith, and Factories — 86
- 3.5 Bridgeton and Dalmarnock: Sport, Steel, and Survival — 91
- 3.6 Tollcross and Shettleston: Garden Suburbs, Swimming Pools, and Working-Class Pride — 97

Chapter 4: The Southside – Identity, Diversity, and Change — 102
- 4.1 Gorbals and Laurieston: Displacement and Design — 102
- 4.2 Tradeston to Kingston: Bridges, Brew Houses and Brutalism — 107
- 4.3 Pollokshields and Govanhill: Glasgow's Global Neighborhoods — 113
- 4.4 Queen's Park, Strathbungo and Shawlands: Southside Soul and Suburbia — 119

Chapter 5: Glasgow Lives – Stories, Struggles, and Strength — 125
- 5.1 Epilogue – The Future of Glasgow: A City Still in the Making — 125
- 5.2 Oral Histories and Local Legends: Listening to the City's Soul — 129
- 5.3 Migrations and Memories: Journeys That Shaped the City — 134
- 5.4 Women of Glasgow: Unheard Voices and Hidden Histories — 139
- 5.5 Activism and Action: From Red Clydeside to Climate Marches — 144

Chapter 6: Glasgow's Hidden Layers – Lost Places, Secret Spaces — 150
- 6.1 Underground Glasgow: Vaults, Tunnels, and Forgotten Foundations — 150
- 6.2 Ghost Signs and Derelict Halls: Faded Echoes in the Urban Fabric — 155
- 6.3 Urban Nature and Wild Corners: Green Pockets and Overgrown Stories — 160
- 6.4 The City After Dark: Glasgow's Nighttime Narratives — 164
- 6.5 The Unseen City: Accessibility, Exclusion, and Inclusion — 169

Chapter 7: Cultural Currents – Glasgow in the Arts and Imagination 175
    7.1 On Screen and Stage: Glasgow in Film, TV, and Theatre 175
    7.2 The Music Walk: Venues, Voices, and Vibrations 178
    7.3 Street Art and Graffiti: Walls That Speak 183
    7.4 Glasgow in Literature: From Alasdair Gray to Modern Memoir 188
    7.5 Museums, Galleries and DIY Spaces: Curating the City 192

Introduction: Walking Glasgow – A City of Layers

Glasgow is a city that reveals itself in layers — a living, breathing urban tapestry stitched together by centuries of transformation, resilience, and reinvention. It is a place where sandstone Victorian grandeur meets post-industrial grit, where leafy boulevards and gritty tenements coexist, where the echoes of shipyard hammers can still be felt beneath the glassy skyline of a city reborn. To walk Glasgow is to walk through time — not just to see the city, but to *feel* it.

This book, **The Complete Walking Guide: Eighteen City Walks from Kelvingrove to the Cathedral, Ashton Lane, and the Waterfront**, is not a conventional guidebook. It's an invitation — to journey beyond postcards and tourist trails, and into the soul of Scotland's largest city. These eighteen curated walks are more than geographic routes; they are narratives, each peeling back a distinct layer of Glasgow's identity. From its medieval heart at High Street to the buzzing multiculturalism of Govanhill, from grand civic architecture to grassroots art collectives in hidden lanes, every street tells a story — and every story offers a window into what makes Glasgow truly unique.

Why Walk Glasgow?

Glasgow is best understood on foot. Unlike cities where historic cores are compact and neatly preserved, Glasgow sprawls — unplanned, chaotic, vital. Its charm lies not in symmetry but in serendipity. You turn a corner and stumble into a Victorian arcade. You pass through a drab corridor and emerge into a sunlit courtyard filled with murals and music. The city speaks softly but insistently through its façades, public art, accents, and contradictions.

To walk Glasgow is to bear witness — to its triumphs and wounds, its ongoing fight for identity, justice, and dignity. You walk not just across physical ground, but across epochs: the ecclesiastical power of the medieval bishopric; the mercantile wealth of the 18th century tobacco lords; the industrial supremacy of the shipbuilding boom; the social devastation of deindustrialization; and the cultural resurgence of the 21st century. The city has been shaped as much by its thinkers and architects as by its workers, immigrants, artists, and activists.

A City of Contrasts and Continuity

Glasgow is often reduced to simplistic binaries: East End and West End, grit and glamour, Presbyterian austerity and post-punk creativity. But such dichotomies miss the point. The magic of Glasgow lies in its refusal to conform — in the seamless coexistence of contradiction. The West End may house museums and leafy terraces, but it also cradles protest history and working-class memories. The East End, often caricatured for its poverty, is rich in cultural heritage and community strength. The Southside, once peripheral, is now one of the city's most vibrant and diverse districts. The Clyde — once a cradle of global shipbuilding — is now a site of regeneration, its banks lined with symbols of a city determined to reimagine itself.

Glasgow is also a city of deep-rooted civic pride and humor. Locals are quick to self-deprecate, quicker still to defend their city against any external slight. There's a warmth here — gritty, genuine, and hard-won — that can't be faked or franchised. It comes from a long tradition of solidarity and social struggle, of surviving hardship with resilience and wit. Glasgow has a working-class spine and a poetic soul. It produces engineers and comedians, architects and rappers, social reformers and punk bands.

Structure of This Book

This guide is structured into **four core chapters**, each focused on a geographic quadrant — the City Centre and Clyde Corridor, the West End and Maryhill, the East End, and the Southside. Each chapter contains a sequence of walks, but within each walk is a theme: one might center around immigration, another on public housing, another on art and protest, another on redevelopment. We close with a final chapter looking forward — an epilogue reflecting on where Glasgow is heading.

Each walk is mapped out with a combination of historical background, architectural commentary, cultural insight, and suggested stops — including places to eat, detour, or simply sit and absorb the atmosphere. You'll meet visionaries like Charles Rennie Mackintosh and John Wheatley, but also unnamed dockworkers, suffragettes, trade unionists, and modern-day Glaswegians whose stories are etched into the stones beneath your feet.

This book is for wanderers and thinkers — for curious minds who seek not just to *see* but to *understand*. Whether you're a first-time visitor or a lifelong resident, there is always more of Glasgow to uncover. It is a city that resists finality. Even its ruins breathe potential. Even its silence speaks.

Walking Into Glasgow's Future

As much as this guide is a look into the past, it is also a celebration of what's emerging. From community-led regeneration in Govan to climate-focused urban planning along the Clyde, Glasgow is a city in motion. Young creatives are reclaiming post-industrial spaces. Immigrant communities are reshaping the culinary and cultural landscape. Activists are fighting for housing justice and public access. Artists are painting the walls with stories no textbook could tell.

This isn't nostalgia. It's continuity. Glasgow has always moved forward by looking back — not to remain in the past, but to learn from it. The future of this city depends on remembering what made it, and walking with care into what it will become.

So tie your laces. Open your eyes. And begin to walk.

Welcome to **Glasgow Uncovered**.

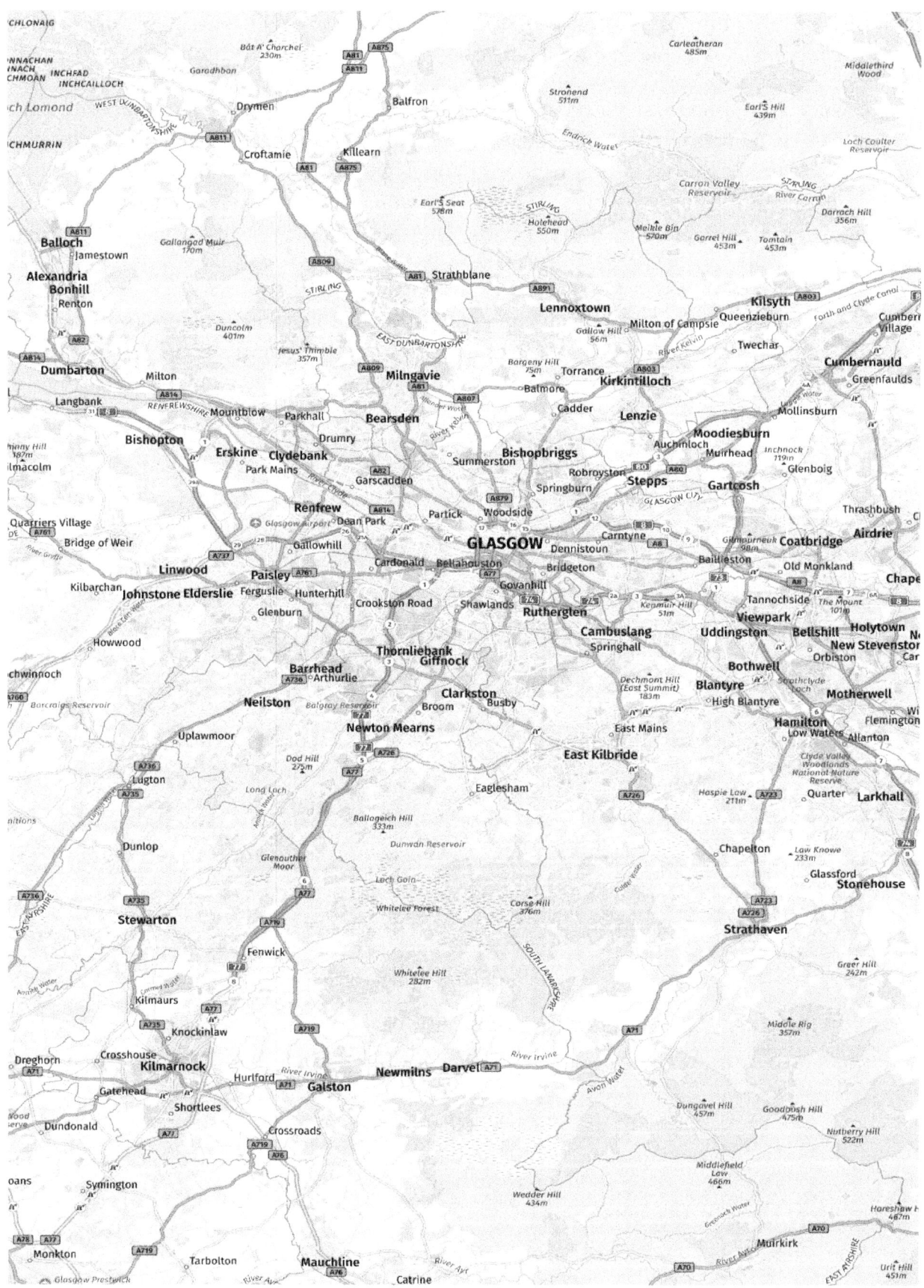

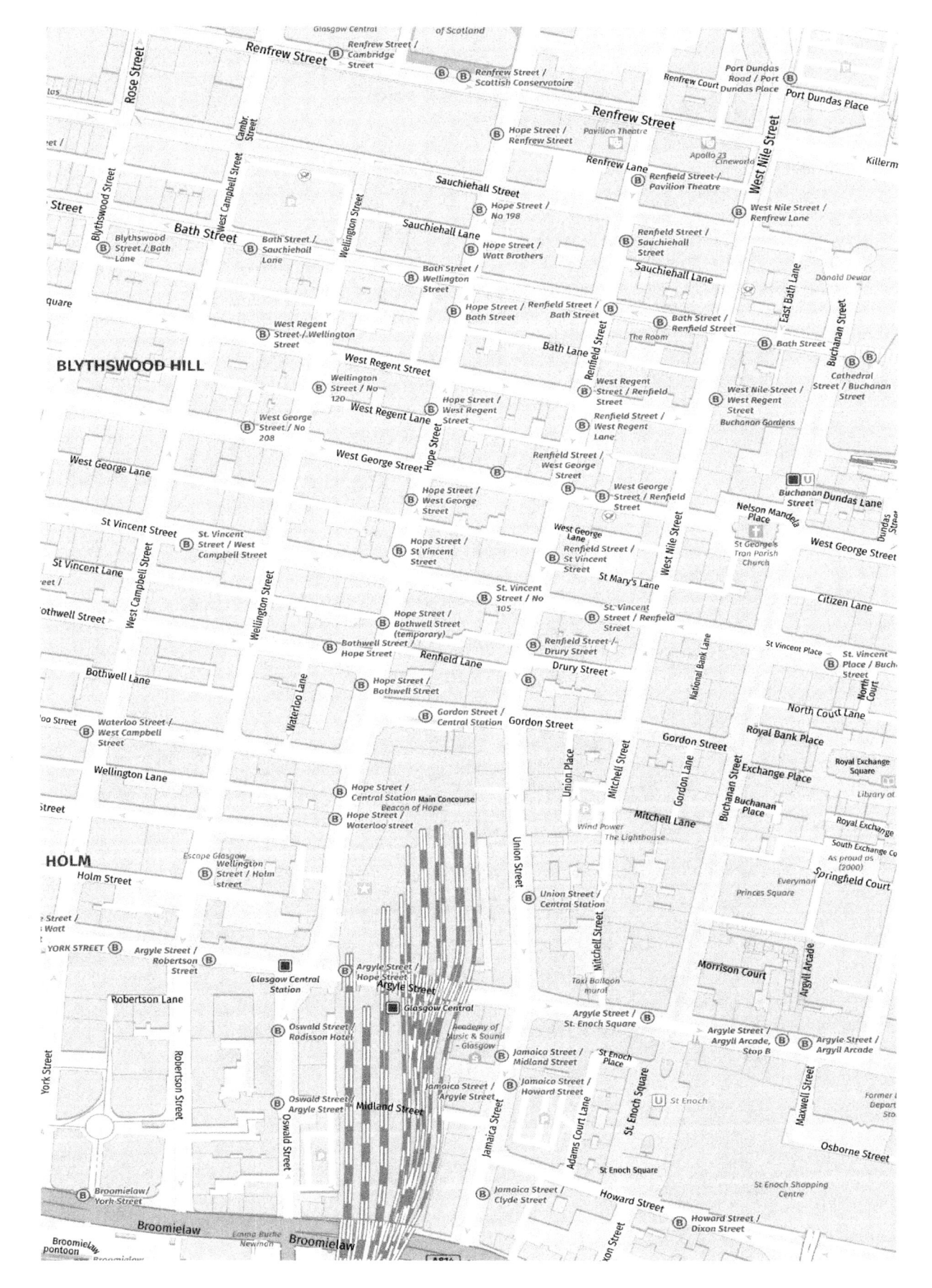

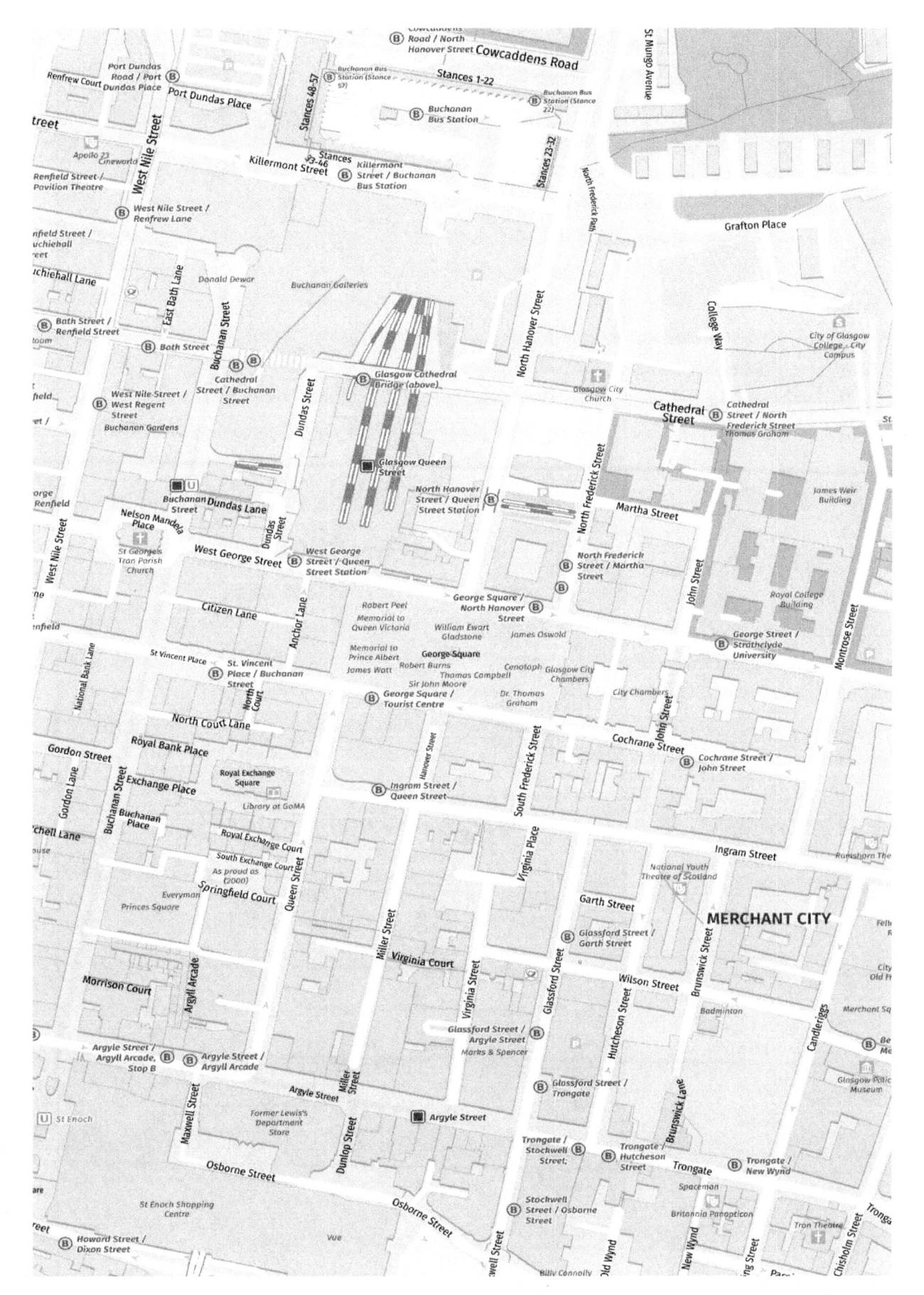

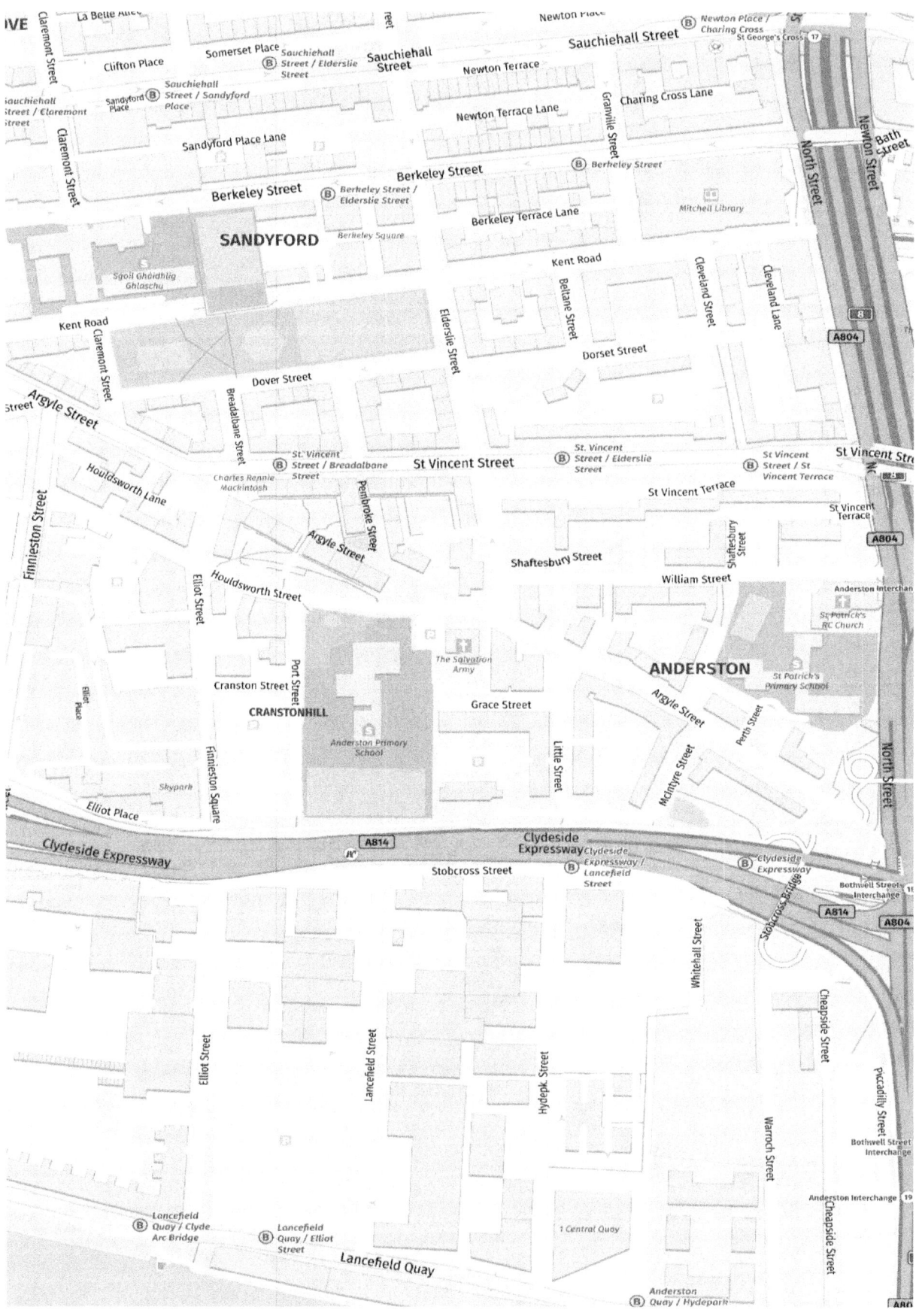

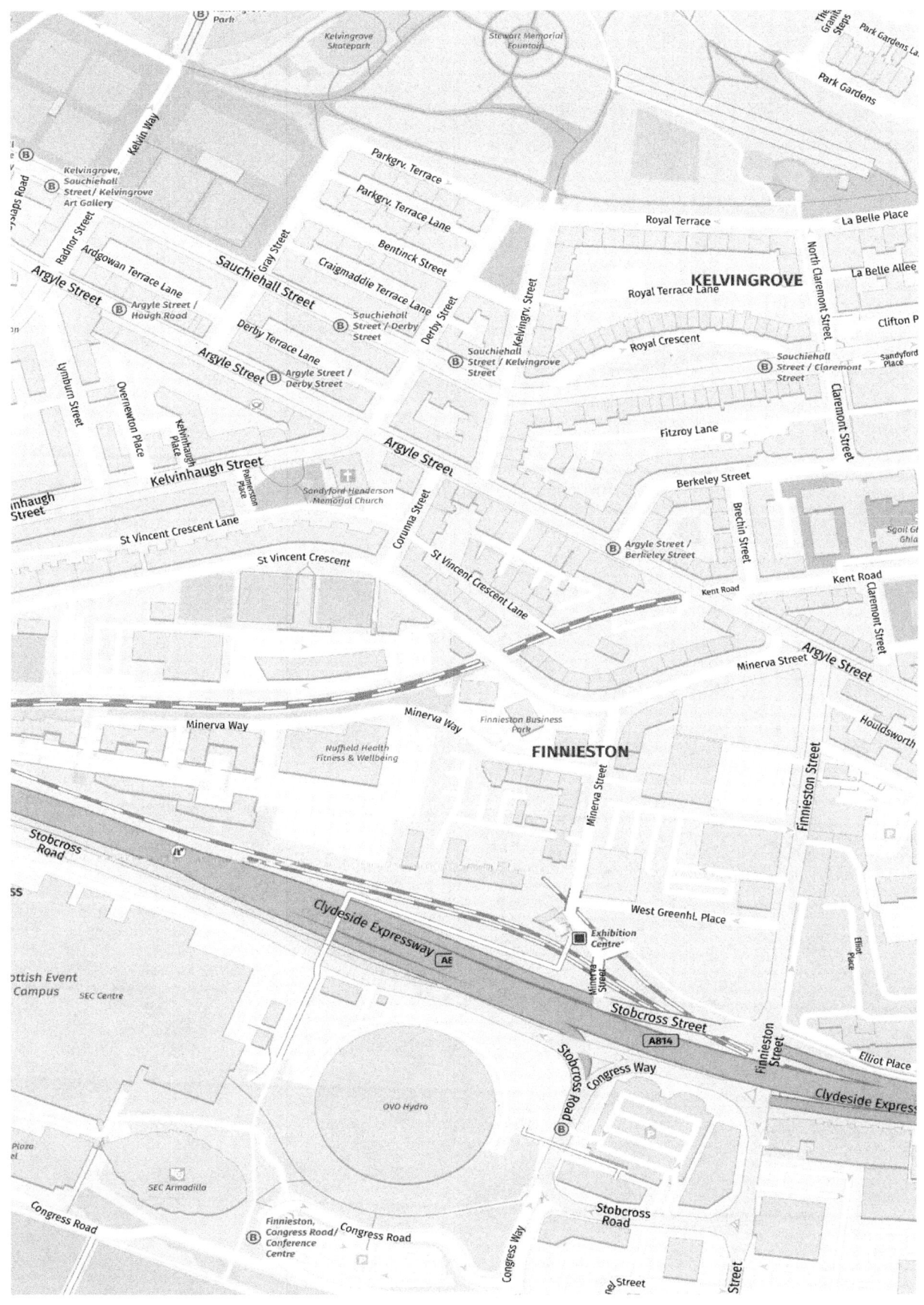

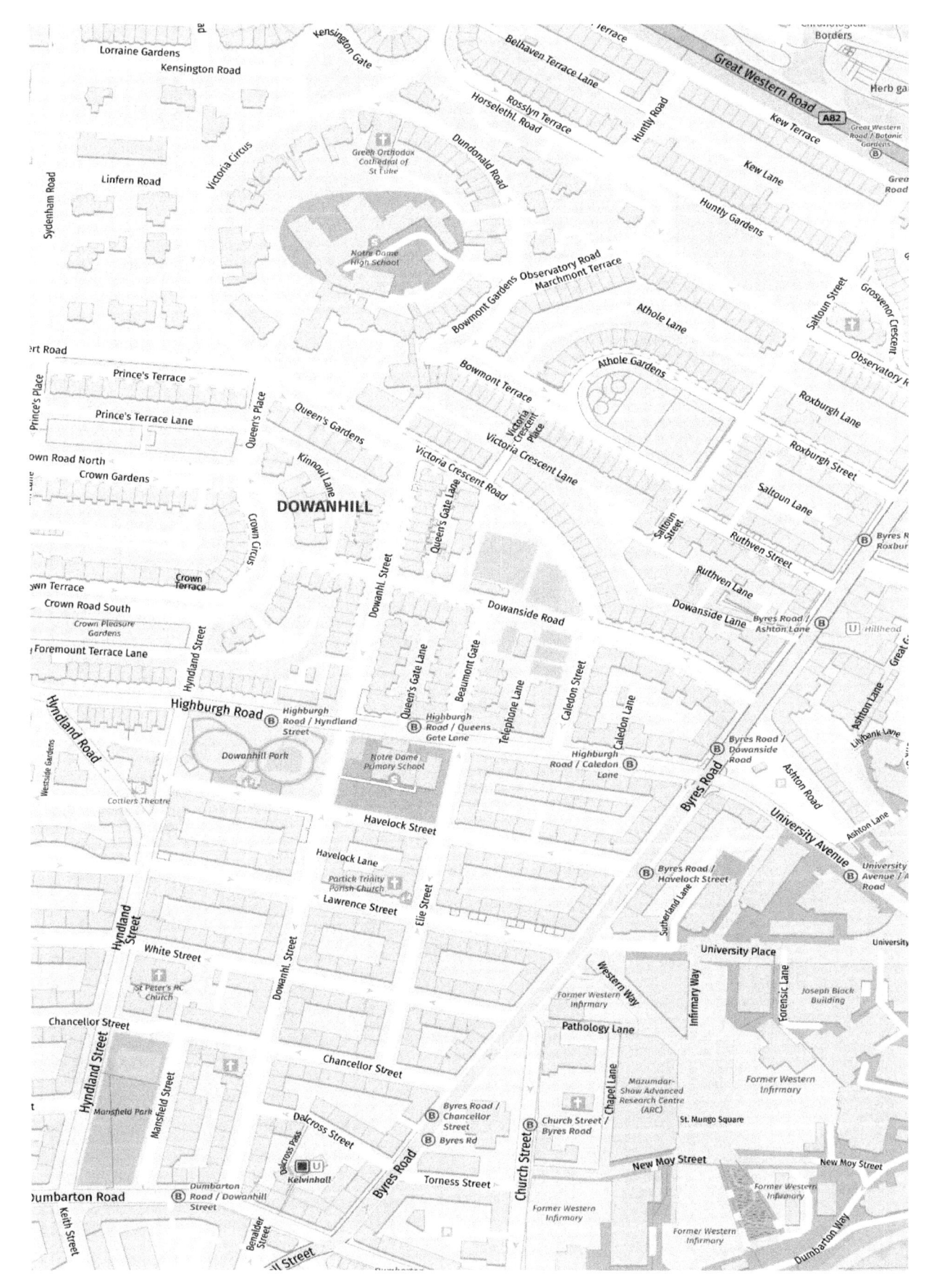

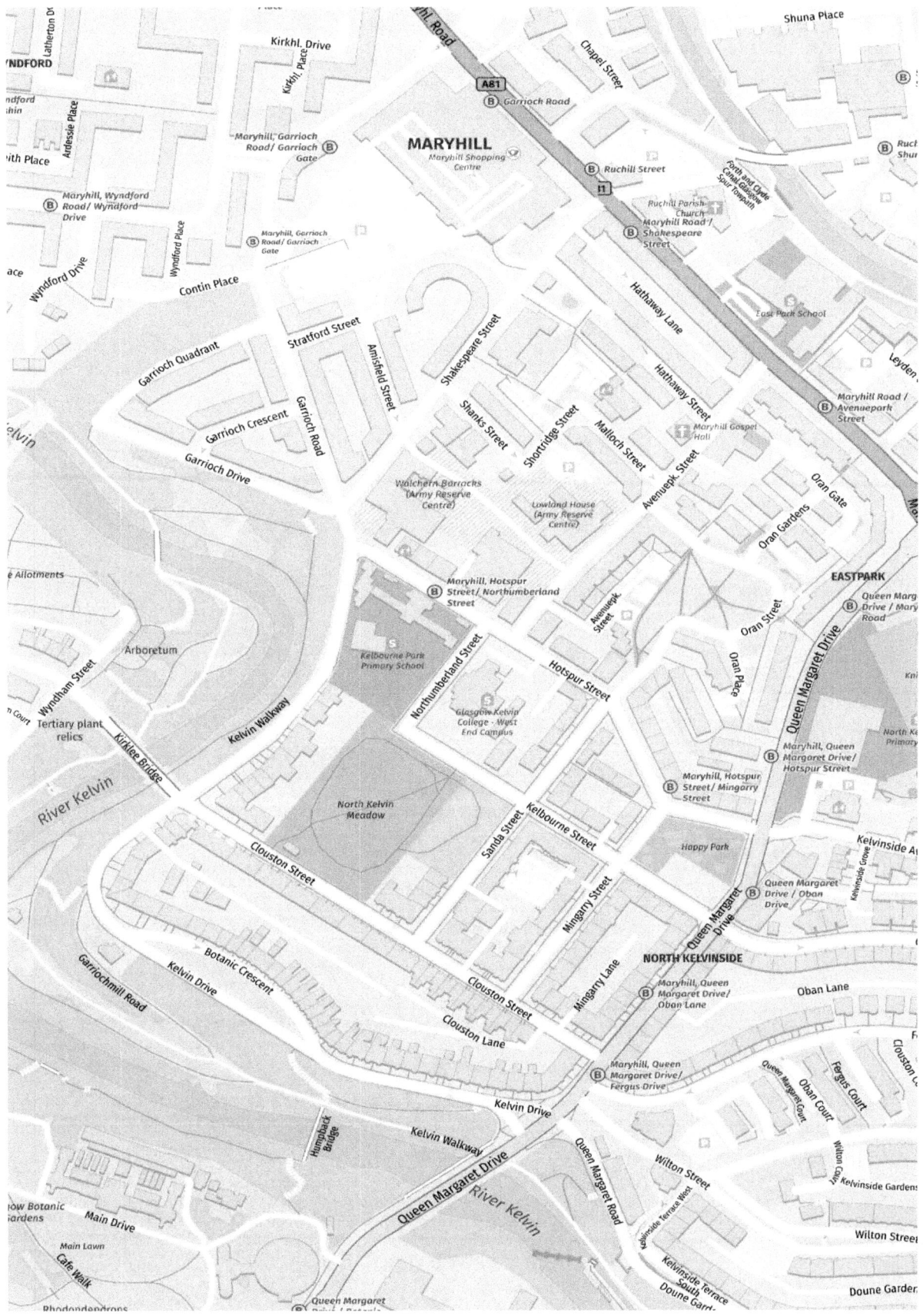

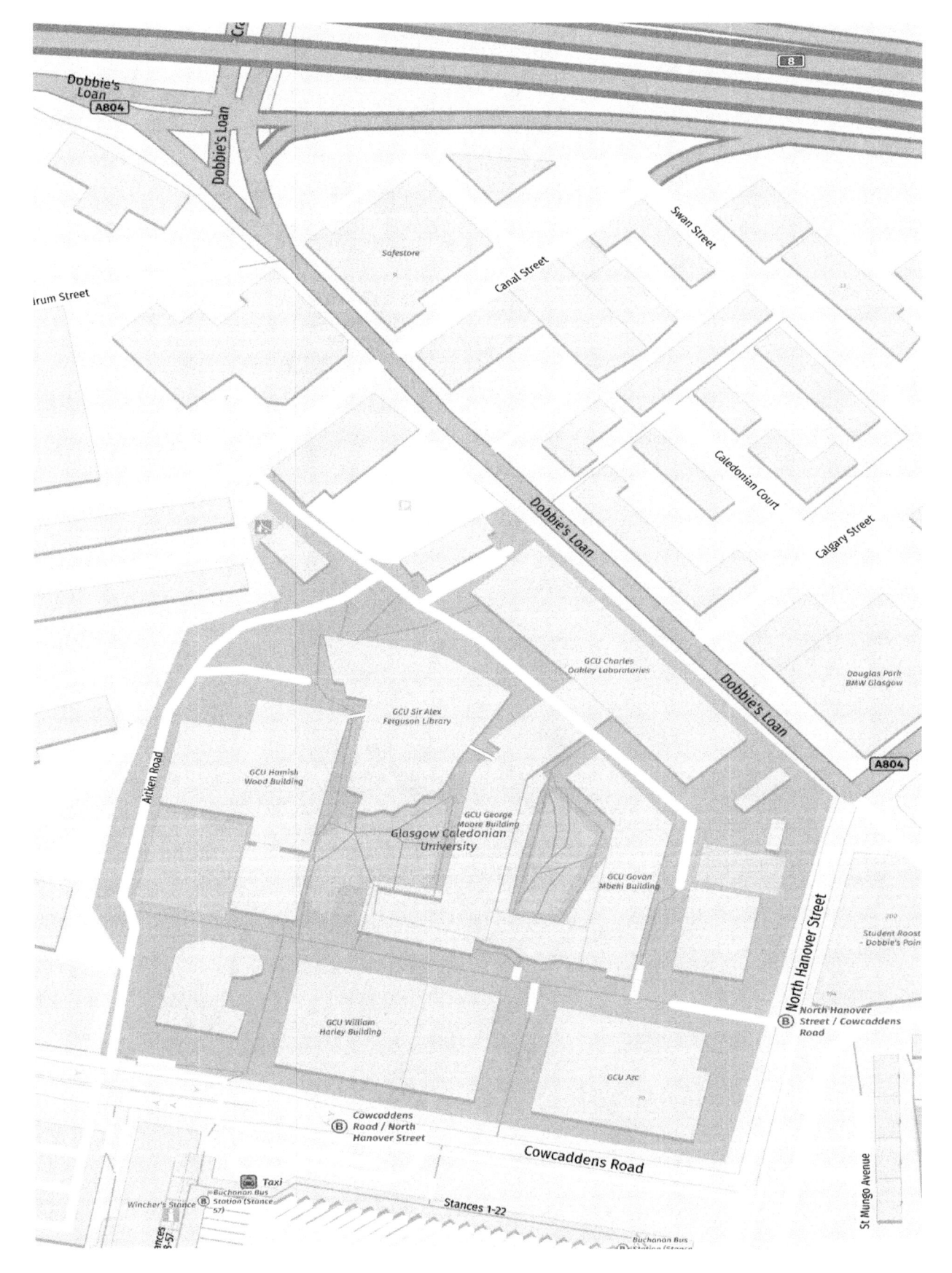

Chapter 1: The Beating Heart - City Centre and the Clyde

1.1 Buchanan Street to George Square: Glasgow's Commercial Pulse

If there is a single corridor in Glasgow where its aspirations, anxieties, wealth, and work ethic collide in one dynamic streetscape, it is Buchanan Street. Paired with George Square at its head and surrounded by a tightly knit matrix of cultural, political, and commercial landmarks, this walk serves as the perfect entry point into the soul of the modern city. It is here that Glasgow's mercantile roots evolve into capitalist sophistication, where Victorian grandeur frames high street fashion, and where public space becomes a stage for everything from silent protests to spontaneous busking.

Beginning at the Argyll Arcade: Where Tradition Meets Luxury

Start your walk at the southern end of Buchanan Street, just off Argyle Street, at the **Argyll Arcade**, one of Britain's oldest covered shopping arcades (1827). Step inside and you're immediately surrounded by glittering window displays of gold and gemstones — this is Glasgow's historic jewellery quarter, and its intricate ironwork and glass ceiling speak of an era when craftsmanship and elegance defined urban design. The arcade feels almost Parisian in layout, echoing 19th-century European passages, and reminds us of Glasgow's international confidence during its commercial boom.

Outside, Buchanan Street begins to rise gently northward — a pedestrianised boulevard flanked by historic sandstone buildings and modern glass façades. The architecture reflects Glasgow's desire to blend old with new, its Victorian civic pride rubbing shoulders with sleek retail modernity.

The Spine of Glasgow: Culture, Commerce, and Contradictions

As you walk up Buchanan Street, you are not merely walking a shopping strip — you are traversing the economic heart of Glasgow. Named after Andrew Buchanan, a tobacco lord whose fortune came from the transatlantic trade (including slavery), the street embodies Glasgow's commercial legacy. Today, this ethical complexity underpins many of the city's heritage sites, urging both recognition and reckoning.

Here, flagship stores from international brands occupy buildings originally built as insurance offices, banks, and gentlemen's clubs. Look up — above the glitzy window displays are pilasters, cornices, and symbolic stone carvings that speak of 19th-century Glasgow's economic might. Notice the street performers: a violinist, a bagpiper, a gravity-defying mime. The street is always alive, not just with commerce, but with expression.

Pause at **House of Fraser** (originally Arthur & Fraser, 1849), Glasgow's most iconic department store, housed in a grand Edwardian building with an ornate terracotta façade. Though it now feels like just another retail outlet, it was once a temple of consumerism for an emerging middle class in industrial Glasgow.

Royal Exchange Square: The Cultural Pivot

Just off Buchanan Street to the east, detour briefly into **Royal Exchange Square**. This neoclassical plaza is dominated by the **Gallery of Modern Art (GoMA)**, formerly the mansion of a tobacco magnate turned Exchange building. The GoMA today stands as a symbol of reclamation — a space once associated with wealth derived from exploitation now redefined as a home for diverse, radical, contemporary art.

Outside, you'll notice the statue of the Duke of Wellington wearing a traffic cone on his head — not vandalism, but a beloved Glaswegian in-joke that has become an unofficial symbol of the city's irreverence. It's a snapshot of the local spirit: wry, clever, and unwilling to defer to authority for the sake of appearances.

The square's symmetry and elegance are surrounded by cafés, bars, and galleries — a reminder that Glasgow's city centre is not just a marketplace but also a meeting ground for ideas, conversation, and protest.

The Artery to the City's Mind: Glasgow's Subway Loop

Beneath your feet lies part of the historic **Glasgow Subway**, the third-oldest underground railway in the world (1896), affectionately known as "The Clockwork Orange." The Buchanan Street Subway Station is a vital artery for students, professionals, and tourists, connecting this dense commercial hub to the intellectual and cultural zones of the West End and Southside.

This subterranean system is a metaphor for Glasgow itself: compact, cyclical, efficient, and always in motion beneath the surface of everyday life.

Theatres and Towers: Art and Ambition Collide

Keep walking north and glance to your right — you'll see **Theatre Royal** on Hope Street, Glasgow's oldest performance venue, and the modern **Scottish Opera HQ**. The performing arts have long thrived here, and Glasgow has earned its title as a UNESCO City of Music for good reason. From the Royal Scottish National Orchestra to indie gigs in underground clubs, creativity pulses in every brick.

As you near the top of Buchanan Street, modern office towers begin to appear — a visual cue that Glasgow remains a working city. The buzz of finance and corporate life hums here, though often in buildings that once housed newspapers, guilds, or union offices. There's always a dialogue between past and present in Glasgow — and rarely a clean separation.

George Square: The Civic Heart of Glasgow

The walk culminates at **George Square**, Glasgow's most important public space. Laid out in 1781 and named after King George III, it is framed by monumental buildings such as the **Glasgow City Chambers**, a marvel of Victorian municipal architecture opened in 1888. The City Chambers is often compared to palaces, and its opulent marble interiors reflect a time when civic power was a source of local pride, not political suspicion.

The square itself is home to statues of Scottish literary and political figures, including Robert Burns, James Watt, and Sir Walter Scott. But George Square is not just for commemorating — it is where Glaswegians gather to protest, celebrate, and mourn. From anti-Iraq War demonstrations to climate rallies, from Hogmanay concerts to vigils, this space is a public conscience.

Look east and you'll see **Queen Street Station**, a major transport hub that feeds the city with movement. Look west, and you'll spot the start of **St Vincent Street**, leading toward the financial district — an area now rebranded as the "International Financial Services District." This juxtaposition of civic grandeur, mass transit, and economic ambition defines Glasgow's centre.

Suggested Stops for the Curious Walker

- **Willow Tea Rooms (Mackintosh at the Willow)** on nearby Sauchiehall Street – a chance to explore Charles Rennie Mackintosh's vision of design as harmony.
- **Cafe Gandolfi** in the Merchant City – a longtime haunt for artists and intellectuals.
- **The Lighthouse** on Mitchell Lane – Scotland's Centre for Design and Architecture, with rooftop views over the city.
- **James Watt College Building** – once part of a technical education revolution that made Glasgow a hub for engineering.

Reflections

This walk, though relatively short in distance, is monumental in meaning. Buchanan Street to George Square is more than a retail spine or civic promenade — it's a theatre where Glasgow performs its identity every day. It encapsulates contradictions: wealth and precarity, progress and memory, spectacle and substance. To walk this stretch is to understand why Glaswegians say: *People Make Glasgow* — because in this pulsing city centre, the people are both audience and actor in a continuous urban story.

1.2 Merchant City – From Tobacco Lords to Creative Quarters

1.2.1 Introduction: A District of Layers

The Merchant City is a district unlike any other in Glasgow — a place where wealth and art, colonialism and commerce, opulence and obscurity collide. Today it's known for cobbled streets, upscale boutiques, buzzing cafés, cutting-edge galleries, and an unmistakable cosmopolitan charm. But underneath the elegance lies a complex legacy — one rooted in the vast fortunes of the 18th-century tobacco trade and built, in part, on the exploitation of enslaved labor abroad.

Named for the tobacco, sugar, linen, and cotton merchants who laid the foundations of Glasgow's economic power during the 18th and 19th centuries, the Merchant City has undergone a profound transformation. Once the home of vast warehouses, counting houses, private banks, and elite residences, it became neglected by the mid-20th century — only to be revived in recent decades as the city's creative and cultural hub.

To walk through the Merchant City today is to step through centuries of ambition, reinvention, and reckoning. It is a walk that demands both admiration and reflection — for this is Glasgow at its most contradictory and, arguably, its most compelling.

1.2.2 The Origins: Glasgow's Mercantile Rise

Glasgow's transformation from a modest market town to a global trading powerhouse began in the early 18th century. With the Act of Union in 1707, Scottish merchants were granted access to England's growing empire. Glasgow's proximity to the Atlantic Ocean — via the River Clyde — gave it a logistical edge, and the city's entrepreneurial elite took full advantage.

The "Tobacco Lords," as they became known, built direct trade links with American colonies, importing enormous quantities of tobacco and later sugar, rum, cotton, and other commodities. Unlike merchants in Bristol or Liverpool who acted more as intermediaries, Glasgow's Tobacco Lords dealt directly with producers and planters — eliminating middlemen and increasing profits.

Men like John Glassford, William Cunninghame, and Alexander Speirs were not just wealthy; they were among the richest individuals in Britain. Glassford alone owned more than 20 ships and had financial stakes in plantations in Virginia and Maryland. These were fortunes built on colonial trade, and much of that trade was inextricably tied to slavery — whether through direct plantation ownership or commercial interdependence.

The new wealth fueled a rapid expansion of the city. The grid-like street pattern of what is now the Merchant City was laid out to accommodate elegant townhouses, counting houses, and financial institutions. The district became the commercial and social epicenter of 18th-century Glasgow — and a symbol of its ambition to rival London and Edinburgh.

1.2.3 Mapping the Past: Street Names, Statues, and Shadows

Even today, the legacy of the merchant elite is written into the geography of the district. Names like Glassford Street, Ingram Street, Cochrane Street, and Buchanan Street all honor prominent merchants. Each of these individuals contributed to the city's infrastructure and civic life, but their wealth was often intertwined with slavery and colonial exploitation.

On Glassford Street once stood Glassford's Mansion — a grand estate said to rival the royal residences of Edinburgh. Though the original building is long gone, it stood as a symbol of wealth accumulated through transatlantic commerce and slave labor. Similarly, Tobacco Merchants House on Miller Street remains one of the few surviving townhouses of that era, and it offers rare architectural insight into the lavish lifestyle of the city's elite.

Other names — Virginia Street, Jamaica Street — reveal even more direct colonial connections. These were not abstract references. They were literal maps of the wealth pipeline: from American plantations to Clyde docks to merchant counting rooms.

While the city is only recently beginning to acknowledge these historical ties in public discourse, activists and historians have called for a deeper, more permanent reckoning — one that includes memorials, educational initiatives, and inclusive storytelling. The Merchant City walk offers an ideal space for this reflection.

1.2.4 Architectural Elegance: Palaces of Commerce and Power

One of the most striking features of the Merchant City is its architectural grandeur. From Georgian townhouses to Victorian arcades, the buildings here tell their own story of wealth and aspiration.

Key landmarks include:

- **The Corinthian Club** – Originally constructed as the Glasgow and Ship Bank in 1842, this neoclassical masterpiece later housed the city's judiciary courts. Its lavish interiors — complete with chandeliers, grand staircases, and domed ceilings — reflect the district's elite aspirations. Today, it functions as a luxury dining and event space.

- **The Italian Centre** – Formerly a warehouse, now a fashion and dining complex, this structure exemplifies the adaptive reuse that characterizes

Merchant City's modern rebirth.

- **Virginia Court and Virginia Galleries** – These tucked-away courtyards and alleyways once housed tobacco and sugar importers; today, they feature boutique retail, hidden cafés, and design studios. The contrast between past and present is stark and thought-provoking.

- **City Halls and the Old Fruitmarket** – These two connected venues represent a transition from commerce to culture. Once places of public assembly and wholesale trading, they now serve as performance venues for orchestras, concerts, and festivals.

Every brick and cornice in the Merchant City seems to whisper of past glories, and yet the district is far from frozen in time.

1.2.5 Decline and Revival: The 20th Century Reimagining

By the 1960s, the grandeur of Merchant City had faded. Suburbanization, deindustrialization, and a lack of urban investment turned the district into a shadow of its former self. Warehouses sat empty. Streets were quiet. Many buildings faced demolition.

However, in the 1980s and 1990s, Glasgow began to reimagine its identity. As part of its campaign to become a "City of Culture," the local council and private developers invested heavily in urban regeneration. The plan: turn derelict spaces into a cultural and creative quarter.

This wasn't merely a facelift. It was a conscious rebranding of the city itself — from industrial powerhouse to cultural capital. Merchant City became the face of this transformation.

Today, walking down its streets, you'll find:

- **Contemporary art galleries** like Transmission and Street Level Photoworks
- **Artists' studios** such as those in the Briggait — a converted 19th-century fish market now hosting over 100 creatives
- **The Tron Theatre**, an icon of progressive Scottish theatre housed in a former 17th-century church
- **Design shops, architecture firms, artisan cafés, and performance spaces** all housed in buildings that once counted ships and cargo

Merchant City's revival is often hailed as one of Glasgow's urban success stories. Yet, it also raises questions about gentrification, affordability, and the future of the working-class communities who once populated nearby tenements.

1.2.6 The Creative Present: Arts, Culture, and Public Life

Merchant City is now arguably Glasgow's most dynamic cultural quarter. It hosts major festivals, public art installations, and experimental theatre productions. Creativity is the new currency.

- **Merchant City Festival** – A multi-day celebration of street performance, theatre, music, design, and food that draws thousands each summer and animates the district with color and vibrancy.

- **Cultural Institutions** – Places like GoMA (Gallery of Modern Art), housed in the former townhouse of a slave-owning merchant, continue the dialogue between past and present by featuring art that often explores themes of empire, identity, and justice.

- **Public Art and Reclaimed Spaces** – Look for murals, sculptures, and installations that quietly provoke — offering everything from political commentary to whimsical visual storytelling.

The balance between heritage and reinvention is ongoing. Merchant City does not just display culture — it debates it.

1.2.7 Food, Drink, and Urban Leisure: A New Social Scene

One of the most visible signs of the district's transformation is its thriving food and drink scene. From independent coffee shops to award-winning restaurants, Merchant City has become a gastronomic hub.

- **The Spanish Butcher**, **Paesano Pizza**, and **Mharsanta** celebrate both local and international cuisine.
- Hidden venues like **Tabac**, **Brutti Compadres**, or **Bar Soba** bring energy to even the narrowest lanes.

Dining here is more than just a transaction — it's social theatre. It reflects the city's diversity, its culinary curiosity, and its growing middle class.

The cafés double as co-working spaces. The restaurants often support local sourcing. Even cocktail menus reference Scotland's whisky heritage. The Merchant City lifestyle is aspirational — but it also seeks to be authentic and inclusive.

1.2.8 Conclusion: Memory and Meaning in the Merchant City

Merchant City is not simply a place on a map. It is a living archive — of wealth and work, of elegance and exploitation, of art and activism. It is a district that demands attention not just for its beauty, but for its truths.

To walk here is to confront Glasgow's global ties — both celebrated and contested. It's to admire architecture while asking who built it. It's to sip artisan coffee in a building that once held enslaved profits. It's to enjoy theatre and design in spaces once ruled by men who trafficked in human capital.

But it is also a space of reinvention. Of artists reclaiming disused spaces. Of communities challenging historical amnesia. Of creativity rising from ruins.

Merchant City is not perfect. But in its complexity lies its power. And in its streets, the past and future of Glasgow meet — not always comfortably, but necessarily.

1.3 Sauchiehall Street and Garnethill: Culture, Nightlife, and Creativity

1.3.1 Introduction: A Walk Through Glasgow's Soul

Sauchiehall Street and Garnethill are more than mere areas of Glasgow—they are vital expressions of the city's ever-changing cultural and social identity. This chapter is a walk through contradiction and complexity: from high street hustle to artistic havens, from historic grandeur to late-night chaos, from quiet synagogues to rowdy clubs, from the visionary mind of Charles Rennie Mackintosh to the thumping beats of The Garage.

Here, the past does not sleep; it pulses through the architecture, the venues, the pavements. Garnethill, perched on its hillside overlooking the urban melee, whispers stories of activism, education, migration, and spirituality. Sauchiehall Street, below, shouts — a riot of neon, noise, crowds, and creativity. Together, they form a compelling narrative arc about what Glasgow has been and what it continues to become.

This chapter will guide you through Sauchiehall Street's historical evolution, cultural landmarks, musical legacies, and urban challenges. Then, you will ascend to Garnethill, to uncover layers of architectural vision, Jewish heritage, radical politics, and quiet introspection. By the end, you'll not only have walked the streets — you'll have walked into the essence of Glasgow itself.

1.3.2 The Rise of Sauchiehall Street: From Willow Fields to Electric Avenue

The name "Sauchiehall" is derived from the Scots words *sauchie haugh* — meaning "willow meadow." In the 18th century, this area was still pastoral, lying on the edges of Glasgow's growing core. By the early 19th century, the expansion of the city's wealthy mercantile class began pushing westward, transforming Sauchiehall into a fashionable residential street lined with Georgian villas and townhouses.

As the 1800s progressed, commercial ambition reshaped the area. Department stores arrived—Copland & Lye, Pettigrew & Stephens, and others—offering luxurious shopping experiences for an increasingly aspirational middle class. Elegant tearooms, hotels, and theatres followed. By the dawn of the 20th century, Sauchiehall Street had become one of the city's most prestigious thoroughfares. Lit by early electric lights, it symbolised Glasgow's modernity, optimism, and cosmopolitan ambition.

1.3.3 Department Stores and Tea Rooms: The Feminised Cityscape

One of the most enduring legacies of Sauchiehall Street is its role in shaping public space for women. In a city once dominated by masculine spheres of industry, the rise of department stores and tea rooms marked a new chapter. They created respectable spaces for women to shop, meet, and socialise outside the home.

The **Willow Tea Rooms**, designed by Charles Rennie Mackintosh in 1903 for businesswoman Kate Cranston, are iconic. Located at 217 Sauchiehall Street, the tearoom was both a commercial and artistic triumph. Mackintosh's designs reflected Glasgow Style modernism — full of geometric grace, symbolic detail, and aesthetic unity. Today, a restored version of the tearoom continues to draw admirers from around the world.

These spaces were revolutionary in subtle ways — allowing women more visibility and autonomy within the city. In this way, Sauchiehall became not just a shopping district, but a social experiment in progress.

1.3.4 The Golden Age of Entertainment: Cinemas, Theatres, and Music Halls

From the late 19th century into the mid-20th century, Sauchiehall Street became Glasgow's entertainment hub. It was home to numerous theatres, music halls, and cinemas that catered to all classes. Few streets in Scotland could rival its density of venues.

The Pavilion Theatre, opened in 1904, still operates as one of Scotland's most beloved performance spaces, famed for pantomime, variety shows, and comedy acts. Nearby, the **Empire Theatre**, **Lyric Theatre**, and **Alhambra Theatre** once boomed with vaudeville acts, singers, and early film screenings. Though many of these venues no longer exist, their legacy lives on in the city's continued love for live performance.

In the 20th century, the rise of cinema gave Sauchiehall a new identity. Art Deco-style picture houses like the **La Scala** and **Green's Playhouse** — once the largest cinema in Europe with over 4,300 seats — became temples of escape for working-class Glaswegians. Green's later transformed into the **Apollo**, a legendary concert venue that hosted everyone from David Bowie to The Rolling Stones.

1.3.5 Nightlife and Subculture: The Garage, ABC, and Sleazy's

As retail faded in prominence in the late 20th century, Sauchiehall Street evolved once again — this time into Glasgow's nightlife capital. The 1980s and 1990s saw the rise of the city's student population and indie culture, giving way to a more hedonistic, creative, and rebellious vibe.

The Garage, opened in 1994, is still running strong today as one of the UK's most iconic student nightclubs. It boasts multiple rooms, foam parties, and a reputation for wild nights. Nearby, **Nice 'N' Sleazy** remains a treasured haunt for live music lovers, poets, DJs, and misfits. Its red neon glow is a kind of pilgrimage marker for alternative Glaswegians.

Further along, **ABC (O2 ABC)** emerged as a key live venue before it was tragically gutted by fire in 2018. Its legacy remains in the memories of countless gigs and sweaty dance nights.

Though club culture in Glasgow has faced threats from gentrification, licensing restrictions, and shifting habits, Sauchiehall Street still pulses after dark. It's less glamorous than in its heyday, but it remains a place of energy and experimentation — especially for those seeking a night that defies predictability.

1.3.6 Garnethill: A Hill of Visionaries and Activists

Garnethill rises just north of Sauchiehall Street — a residential hill that feels like another world. Here, the city quiets. Townhouses from the 19th century line steep cobbled streets. From the top, panoramic views stretch across Glasgow's skyline. But Garnethill is more than peaceful—it's powerful.

This was Glasgow's first true Jewish neighbourhood. Immigrants fleeing pogroms in Eastern Europe found a haven here in the late 1800s. Their cultural and religious heart was the **Garnethill Synagogue**, built in 1879 — the oldest in Scotland. Designed in a mix of Romanesque and Byzantine styles, it still serves a small congregation and is home to the **Scottish Jewish Archives Centre**.

Garnethill was also home to the early feminist and suffragette movements, radical student activism, and later, LGBTQ+ advocacy. Its narrow streets have been walked by artists, anarchists, rabbis, and refugees alike.

1.3.7 The Glasgow School of Art: Mackintosh's Monument

No visit to Garnethill is complete without standing before the **Glasgow School of Art**. Founded in 1845, the school became world-famous thanks to Charles Rennie Mackintosh's 1897–1909 masterpiece, the Mackintosh Building. It was not just a school; it was a manifesto. Mackintosh blended Scottish baronial style with art nouveau elegance and modernist abstraction.

Two devastating fires — one in 2014 and a second in 2018 — gutted the building, raising heartbreaking questions about cultural preservation, identity, and continuity. As of 2025, plans for reconstruction are ongoing, with the goal of restoring it as closely as possible to Mackintosh's vision using original materials and techniques.

The GSA remains one of the most respected art schools in the world. Its alumni list includes internationally acclaimed creatives across visual art, design, architecture, and film. Its presence gives Garnethill an atmosphere of quiet creativity, intellectual intensity, and global ambition.

1.3.8 Contemporary Renewal: The Avenues Project and Future Visions

Glasgow has not abandoned Sauchiehall Street. Far from it. In recent years, the **Avenues Project** has pumped millions into redesigning parts of the city centre, with Sauchiehall Street as a pilot. Wider pavements, bike lanes, tree planting, and improved lighting were intended to reframe the street as a civic space rather than just a transit zone or commercial strip.

Reception has been mixed. Some see improvement; others lament the lack of bold vision. What's certain is that Sauchiehall Street remains in flux. The rise of e-commerce, city centre depopulation, and cultural shifts challenge its traditional role. Yet, its cultural DNA — artistic, rebellious, communal — endures.

In Garnethill, the priority is preservation and stewardship. The community has resisted large-scale commercialisation, focusing instead on supporting resident artists, green spaces, and heritage efforts.

1.3.9 Walking It: How to Explore Sauchiehall and Garnethill

Suggested Route:

- Begin at **Charing Cross**, at the western edge of Sauchiehall Street.
- Walk east past **The Garage**, **Nice 'N' Sleazy**, and the remains of **ABC**.
- Pause at the **Willow Tea Rooms** for a glimpse of Mackintosh's legacy.
- Detour north to **Garnethill**, climbing the steps past GSA.
- Visit the **Garnethill Synagogue** and enjoy the view from the park at the hill's crest.
- Descend back to Sauchiehall Street and continue east toward Buchanan Galleries.

Tips:

- Visit during the day for art and history, and return at night if you want to experience the wild, eclectic nightlife.
- Bring a camera: Garnethill's street art, staircases, and vistas are highly photogenic.
- Support local: check out pop-up art galleries, community cafés, and student-run exhibits.

1.3.10 Conclusion: Two Souls, One City

Sauchiehall Street and Garnethill are twins of a kind — different in mood and form, but joined by energy, innovation, and resistance. One is horizontal and loud; the other vertical and contemplative. One thrives on crowds; the other on community. One blares music; the other paints.

To understand Glasgow, you must walk both. In their tension lies the city's identity — messy, creative, rebellious, and always evolving.

1.4 Anderston and Argyle Street: Echoes of Industry and Innovation

1.4.1 Introduction: The Forgotten Heart of Glasgow

Anderston and Argyle Street form one of Glasgow's most historically rich yet often overlooked districts. Tucked between the vibrant city centre and the sprawling West

End, this area has long been a crucible of industry, migration, innovation, and reinvention. Once the thundering hub of shipbuilding, rail engineering, and warehousing, Anderston bore the smoke-stained soul of the city's industrial revolution. Its streets rang with the clang of hammers and the rumble of carts. Its tenements housed workers from the Highlands, Ireland, and further afield, all drawn by the promise—and burden—of urban life.

Argyle Street, a key artery running through the area, has always been a place of convergence. Historically connecting the city centre to Dumbarton Road and the Clyde's industrial belt, it now bridges past and present—lined with remnants of Victorian ambition, mid-century upheaval, and 21st-century reinvention. Today, the street hums with shops, hotels, cultural institutions, and signs of urban regeneration, but beneath the surface, its layers are many and meaningful.

This chapter explores the intertwined histories of Anderston and Argyle Street—examining their industrial might, their post-war disfigurement, their cultural resilience, and their current reawakening.

1.4.2 Early Foundations: A Village Becomes a Powerhouse

The origins of Anderston date back to the early 18th century, when it was little more than a weaving village situated west of the burgeoning town of Glasgow. In 1725, the Anderson family established the village as part of the Stobcross estate, giving it the name Anderston. What began as a rural outpost with handloom cottages and small markets quickly became subsumed into Glasgow's westward expansion.

By the mid-19th century, Anderston had transformed into a dense, working-class district powered by steam and soot. Its strategic location—near the River Clyde and the rapidly expanding railway network—made it a natural site for factories, foundries, printworks, textile mills, and ship repair yards. Its tenement-lined streets housed thousands of labourers and their families in conditions often described as overcrowded and unsanitary, yet profoundly communal and culturally vibrant.

Argyle Street, which originally followed the line of a Roman road, emerged as Anderston's commercial spine, connecting Glasgow's medieval centre with the Clyde's industrial west. By the 1800s, it was lined with inns, workshops, and ironmongers—an urban seam binding together trade, travel, and toil.

1.4.3 The Shipyards and Railway Legacy

Anderston's proximity to the Clyde made it a cornerstone of Glasgow's shipbuilding empire. Though not home to major yards like Govan or Scotstoun, the district was a vital node in the maritime supply chain. It housed warehouses, marine engineering shops, ropeworks, and metal-bashing factories that produced everything from anchors to boiler plates.

Equally vital was its role in rail engineering. The **Anderston Cross railway station**, opened in 1896, connected the area to the suburban and intercity network. Nearby, **Stobcross goods yard**—a massive freight hub—channelled raw materials and finished goods in and out of the city. These infrastructures were arteries of empire, feeding Glasgow's economic might across oceans and borders.

The rumble of trains and steam engines, the cries of dockers and foremen, and the acrid scent of coal and iron were the daily atmosphere of Anderston—a living, breathing machine of industrial civilisation.

1.4.4 Social Fabric: Tenements, Taverns, and Trade Unionism

Life in Anderston was intense, communal, and politically charged. Its dense tenements, many built hastily to accommodate surging populations, became microcosms of working-class resilience. Extended families lived cheek-by-jowl in single-end flats. Shared washhouses (commonly known as "closes") fostered gossip, solidarity, and sometimes conflict. It was in these spaces that Glasgow's reputation as the "Red Clydeside" began to take shape.

The early 20th century saw Anderston emerge as a hotbed of trade union activity and labour rights agitation. Dockworkers, printers, and railwaymen often led strikes and demonstrations from the area. Taverns doubled as unofficial political clubs. Socialists and syndicalists debated revolution over pints and pamphlets. During the 1919 Battle of George Square—when striking workers clashed with police and troops—Anderston supplied many of the marchers.

Though poverty and overcrowding were real, there was a fierce pride in community. People came together through hardship. The area's Irish-Catholic and Scottish-Protestant populations lived in close proximity, often negotiating tension through shared labour and sport.

1.4.5 Destruction and Displacement: The Motorway Cuts Through

Anderston's downfall came not from war but from urban planning. Post-World War II, Glasgow embarked on an ambitious redevelopment program aimed at eradicating slums and modernising infrastructure. Inspired by American urbanism, city officials approved the **Bruce Report**, which called for motorways, high-rise housing, and wholesale demolition of older districts.

From the late 1960s through the 1970s, much of Anderston was razed to the ground. Streets were erased. Tenements were demolished. Communities were scattered to peripheral schemes like Easterhouse, Drumchapel, and Castlemilk. In their place, the **M8 motorway** was driven directly through the heart of the district, severing it physically and emotionally from the city.

The **Anderston Centre**, built in 1972 as a mixed-use megastructure of brutalist towers, shops, offices, and walkways, was meant to replace the lost vibrancy. But it soon fell into neglect—plagued by crime, emptiness, and structural decay. What was intended as a utopia became a symbol of architectural and social failure.

Argyle Street, once continuous, was split in two. The western segment declined sharply, its shopfronts shuttered and its foot traffic diverted. Anderston's identity was broken—its past buried under concrete and traffic fumes.

1.4.6 Cultural Resilience: Music, Art, and the Hidden Underground

Despite—or perhaps because of—the trauma of redevelopment, Anderston has remained a site of cultural resistance and experimentation. In the 1980s and 1990s, unused buildings and forgotten corners became homes to underground music scenes, squatter art projects, and alternative nightlife.

The **Argyle Street Arches**, located under the railway lines at Glasgow Central Station, became an unlikely hub of club culture. Known simply as "The Arches," the venue hosted everything from avant-garde theatre to world-class DJs. It was a melting pot of techno, industrial, house, and performance art, helping define Glasgow's reputation as a creative powerhouse. Though the venue closed in 2015, its legacy continues in Glasgow's electronic music scene.

Elsewhere, small galleries and artist studios took root in the interstices. Community arts groups worked to reclaim public space and restore memory to a neighbourhood long denied its past. Murals, installations, and oral history projects have all played a role in this quiet resurrection.

1.4.7 Regeneration and Reconnection: The New Anderston

Beginning in the early 2000s, a wave of regeneration efforts sought to heal Anderston's wounds. The **Anderston Regeneration Masterplan**, led by Sanctuary Housing and Glasgow City Council, involved the demolition of dilapidated high-rises and the construction of new low-rise housing designed with community in mind. Streets were reconnected. The area's human scale was slowly restored.

The **Anderston Footbridge**, completed in 2013, physically and symbolically reconnected the district across the M8 motorway—linking it once again to the city centre. Green spaces, public art, and modern flats replaced some of the previous blight. New hotels, restaurants, and office buildings now cluster around **Blythswood Court** and the **International Financial Services District (IFSD)** near the river, reflecting Glasgow's post-industrial pivot toward finance and tourism.

Argyle Street itself has seen selective revitalisation. Trendy eateries, boutique shops, and pedestrian-friendly initiatives aim to restore its stature. Yet inequalities remain. Housing insecurity, social fragmentation, and gentrification pose fresh challenges.

1.4.8 Notable Landmarks and Cultural Sites

- **Anderston Parish Church**: A contemporary Presbyterian church with striking architecture, rooted in a tradition of community care and social justice.
- **Argyle Street Arches (Platform)**: Though The Arches venue is gone, the redeveloped space known as Platform now hosts food markets, events, and festivals under the railway tracks.
- **Scottish Exhibition and Conference Centre (SECC)** and **Hydro Arena**: Just south of Anderston, on the banks of the Clyde, these massive venues anchor Glasgow's cultural and event economy. They are modern descendants of the city's industrial exhibitions.
- **St Vincent Street Church**: Designed by Alexander "Greek" Thomson, this 1859 church is one of the finest examples of neoclassical architecture in the UK and a proud symbol of Anderston's former grandeur.

1.4.9 Walking It: Discovering Anderston on Foot

Suggested Route:

- Start at **Buchanan Street**, then head west along **Argyle Street**, passing through the **Arches**.
- Cross under the M8 via the **Anderston Footbridge**.
- Explore the rebuilt **Anderston Centre** and surrounding housing estates.
- Head south toward the river, passing the **IFSD**, then detour to **St Vincent Street Church**.
- End at **Kelvingrove** or loop back eastward to admire how old and new now coexist.

Tips:

- Visit mid-morning for photography and to witness daily life.
- Look for plaques and murals that tell the story of vanished streets and communities.
- Support local businesses in the area's newer developments—they represent the future trying to reclaim the past.

1.4.10 Conclusion: Echoes and Embrace

Anderston and Argyle Street are more than historic footnotes—they are living testaments to Glasgow's cycles of industry, destruction, and reinvention. Their scars are visible, but so is their resilience. In the clang of the past, the hum of modernity, and the whispers of memory, these streets continue to echo with innovation and endurance.

To understand Glasgow, you must walk Anderston—not as it was, but as it is now becoming.

1.5 The Clyde Waterfront: Regeneration and Resilience

1.5.1 Introduction: From Shipyards to Skyline

The Clyde Waterfront, stretching from Glasgow Green to the city's western fringes at the Clyde Tunnel, encapsulates one of the most dramatic urban transformations in contemporary Scotland. Once the beating heart of Glasgow's global industrial prowess—where shipbuilding giants like John Brown and Fairfield launched liners that shaped the world—the River Clyde is now at the centre of a post-industrial rebirth marked by innovation, design, tourism, and cultural resurgence.

In the space of a few decades, rusting cranes and derelict docks have given way to gleaming conference centres, residential developments, waterfront walkways, and cultural icons. Yet this renaissance has not come easily. It is a story of resilience in the face of deindustrialisation, strategic planning after decades of decline, and a city's determination to honour its heritage while forging a sustainable and inclusive future.

This chapter explores the layered identity of the Clyde Waterfront—tracing its industrial legacy, examining key regeneration milestones, highlighting flagship architecture and cultural venues, and assessing the social implications of one of Britain's most ambitious urban renewal projects.

1.5.2 A River of Industry: Clyde's Historical Might

By the late 19th century, the River Clyde had become one of the most famous waterways in the world. Glasgow, once landlocked and modest in scope, had literally reshaped the river—dredging its channel, straightening its course, and deepening its basin—to accommodate massive ocean-going vessels.

This engineering feat transformed the Clyde into the cradle of modern shipbuilding. Iconic vessels like the RMS *Lusitania*, HMS *Hood*, and the QE2 were born in the shipyards of Govan and Clydebank. At its height, the Clyde's banks were lined with foundries, engineering plants, steelworks, and dry docks employing tens of thousands of skilled labourers.

The river was also a gateway for imports and exports: tea from India, coal from Ayrshire, linen and cotton goods from Glasgow's mills. Merchant houses, bonded warehouses, and transport offices sprung up along the Broomielaw and beyond. This industrial juggernaut helped turn Glasgow into the "Second City of the Empire."

But the river was more than an economic engine—it was a cultural and social landscape. Entire communities were built around the docks. Traditions, dialects, and identities formed in the shadow of the cranes. The Clyde was both workplace and stage—a constant presence in the life of Glaswegians.

1.5.3 Collapse and Consequence: Decline in the 20th Century

The post–World War II era brought profound changes. Global competition, the decline of empire, containerisation, and political underinvestment led to the slow, painful erosion of Clyde shipbuilding. One by one, yards closed. Massive employers like Upper Clyde Shipbuilders and Fairfield began laying off workers. By the 1980s, the waterfront had become a landscape of ruin—abandoned hulks, toxic waste, derelict quays, and economic stagnation.

Communities that had once thrived—Govan, Partick, and Linthouse among them—were thrust into unemployment and urban decay. The social consequences were severe: poverty, addiction, population decline, and loss of local identity. For many Glaswegians, the river became a painful symbol of what had been lost.

Efforts at regeneration in the late 20th century were piecemeal and largely ineffective until the early 2000s, when local government, private investors, and UK/EU funding coalesced around a grander vision.

1.5.4 A New Vision: The Clyde Waterfront Regeneration Initiative

Launched formally in 2003, the **Clyde Waterfront Regeneration Project** was a £5.6 billion public-private partnership aimed at revitalising over 20 kilometres of riverfront between Glasgow Green and Dumbarton. The initiative sought to reimagine the Clyde as a place to live, work, invest, and play—not just as an economic zone, but as a livable, attractive urban corridor.

Key goals included:

- Reconnecting the city to the river via public access, promenades, and public transport

- Attracting inward investment in business, media, and finance
- Promoting cultural institutions and events
- Enhancing housing and creating mixed-use developments
- Cleaning up environmental damage and improving flood resilience

This vision was not just about new buildings, but about symbolic healing: reclaiming the river as a shared civic space, not a barrier between neighbourhoods or a relic of industrial trauma.

1.5.5 Architectural Icons and Cultural Anchors

The Clyde Waterfront is now home to some of Glasgow's most recognisable and celebrated buildings—structures that both reflect the city's ambitions and commemorate its past.

The Clyde Auditorium ("The Armadillo")

Designed by Sir Norman Foster, this concert venue opened in 1997 and quickly became one of Glasgow's signature structures. Its overlapping, shell-like forms evoke both modernity and nautical heritage—often likened to a ship's hull or a giant armadillo. The Armadillo is a key component of the Scottish Event Campus (SEC) and regularly hosts musical performances, conferences, and televised events.

The SSE Hydro

Opened in 2013 next to the Armadillo, this striking arena hosts everything from global pop stars to professional wrestling and political summits. Its circular, translucent design lights up in colour at night, becoming a beacon on the Clyde skyline. It can seat over 14,000 and is one of the top-performing arenas in the world by ticket sales.

The Riverside Museum

Designed by Iraqi-British architect Zaha Hadid, the Riverside Museum opened in 2011 at the mouth of the River Kelvin. It replaced the former Museum of Transport and houses over 3,000 objects, including vintage trams, bicycles, locomotives, and even recreated Glasgow streets. Outside, the tall ship *Glenlee*—a fully restored 19th-century barque—sits moored as a floating exhibit.

BBC Scotland and STV Headquarters

On the south bank of the river at Pacific Quay, modern glass-fronted media headquarters now define Glasgow's role in the creative economy. BBC Scotland's building, opened in 2007, serves as a national hub for broadcasting and digital production.

Science Centre and Glasgow Tower

Also on the south bank, the Glasgow Science Centre is a family-friendly educational attraction with interactive exhibits, a planetarium, and an IMAX cinema. Adjacent is the 127-metre Glasgow Tower—the only structure in the world capable of rotating 360 degrees from its base.

1.5.6 Residential Development and Urban Living

One of the regeneration's key objectives was to reintroduce riverside living. Former docklands were cleared and converted into modern apartment complexes—particularly at Lancefield Quay, Finnieston, and the Glasgow Harbour development west of Partick.

These areas blend upscale flats, landscaped esplanades, and cycling paths, often with river views and access to the Clyde Arc ("Squinty Bridge"). While popular among young professionals, these developments have prompted discussion about housing affordability and the displacement of long-standing working-class communities nnearby

1.5.7 Infrastructure and Connectivity

Transport upgrades were essential to unlocking the riverfront's potential. Projects included:

- **Clyde Arc Bridge (2006):** A cable-stayed bridge linking Finnieston with Pacific Quay, visually striking and symbolic of Glasgow's east-west reconnection.
- **Clyde Walkway and National Cycle Route 75:** Continuous riverside paths ideal for walking, jogging, and cycling, linking key landmarks.
- **Fastlink Bus Corridor:** A dedicated bus route improving access between the city centre, SECC, and hospital campuses.
- **Pedestrian Bridges:** Including the Tradeston Bridge ("Squiggly Bridge") connecting Tradeston with Broomielaw and the wider financial district.

These projects have not only reknit neighbourhoods together but helped shift Glasgow toward a greener, more sustainable urban model.

1.5.8 Social Impact and Uneven Regeneration

While the Clyde Waterfront has been hailed as a success in architectural and investment terms, its social outcomes remain mixed. Many critics point to a **"two-speed regeneration"**—with high-end flats and business districts thriving while poorer communities, especially on the south bank (e.g., Govan, Plantation, Ibrox), continue to face unemployment, health disparities, and housing inequality.

Grassroots organisations have stepped in to fill gaps left by top-down planning. Initiatives like **GalGael** in Govan promote community boat-building, heritage skills, and social inclusion. Local history groups, such as the **Govan Stones Project**, work to preserve early medieval relics and increase local pride.

A key ongoing challenge is ensuring that the Clyde's transformation benefits all Glaswegians—not just newcomers or tourists.

1.5.9 Events, Festivals, and Civic Life

The revitalised waterfront now hosts many of Glasgow's major public events:

- **Celtic Connections (Winter):** Though primarily city-centre based, the Clyde venues often host concerts.
- **Riverside Festival (Spring):** An annual electronic music festival held outside the Riverside Museum, drawing international DJs and thousands of attendees.
- **Clyde Waterfront Walks and Tours:** Guided walking tours of the riverside heritage, covering everything from shipbuilding to modern design.

- **Commonwealth Games Legacy (2014):** The river served as a central backdrop for opening ceremonies and events, boosting civic confidence.

The river is once again a gathering place—a setting for shared memory, celebration, and forward-looking ambition.

1.5.10 Conclusion: The Clyde Today—and Tomorrow

The Clyde Waterfront is a mirror of Glasgow itself: gritty and grand, wounded and reborn, anchored in heritage but brimming with future potential. Where ships once launched into the Atlantic, ideas now flow between media hubs, museums, and arenas. Where industry once towered, culture now thrives.

Yet the regeneration of the Clyde is not a finished project. It remains a work in progress—a test of Glasgow's ability to balance economic growth with social justice, architectural ambition with neighbourhood needs, and history with hope.

To walk the Clyde today is to witness the resilience of a city refusing to be defined by its decline. It is to hear the echoes of hammer and forge replaced by conversation and possibility. It is to believe in a future where the river flows not only through Glasgow's geography, but through its soul.

Chapter 2: The Storied West - Wealth, Art, and Activism

2.1 Kelvingrove and the University of Glasgow: Knowledge and Empire

2.1.1 Introduction: The West End's Cultural Powerhouse

If the River Clyde built Glasgow's economy, the West End sculpted its intellectual and artistic soul. Nowhere is this clearer than in the leafy avenues and grand boulevards surrounding **Kelvingrove** and the **University of Glasgow**, where civic pride, academic distinction, and imperial wealth interweave. These neighbouring districts form the nucleus of a storied enclave that showcases Victorian Glasgow's self-assurance, enlightenment values, and sometimes uncomfortable connections to Britain's global empire.

More than a collection of monuments or university buildings, this part of the city pulses with layered meaning: the pursuit of knowledge and social reform; the celebration of art, architecture, and natural beauty; and the legacies of privilege, philanthropy, and colonial entanglement that shaped much of its development.

2.1.2 Kelvingrove Park: Landscape of Leisure and Enlightenment

First laid out in the 1850s by Sir Joseph Paxton (designer of the Crystal Palace in London), **Kelvingrove Park** is the green lung of the West End. Meandering alongside the River Kelvin, its 85 acres of wooded slopes, ornate terraces, fountains, and Victorian cast-iron bridges offer a picturesque retreat from the surrounding urban grid. Paxton's design was not just aesthetic—it was philosophical. Inspired by Romanticism and Enlightenment ideals, it was meant to elevate Glasgow's rising middle classes, encouraging outdoor recreation, moral improvement, and civic togetherness.

Today, the park remains a beloved public space, frequented by joggers, picnickers, students, and musicians. The bandstand, restored in 2014, hosts summer concerts and political rallies. Monuments to political figures—including Lord Kelvin, Thomas Carlyle, and Field Marshal Roberts—dot the park, though their imperial or militaristic associations have drawn scrutiny in recent years. The River Kelvin, once heavily polluted, now supports fish and otters thanks to decades of environmental restoration.

Kelvingrove Park exemplifies 19th-century Glasgow's aspirations to marry urban progress with natural beauty and public health—an idea now renewed by 21st-century sustainability goals.

2.1.3 Kelvingrove Art Gallery and Museum: Empire, Aesthetics, and Accessibility

Opened in 1901 as the centrepiece of the **Glasgow International Exhibition**, **Kelvingrove Art Gallery and Museum** is one of Scotland's most visited free attractions. Its Spanish Baroque Revival facade, constructed from red Locharbriggs sandstone, was deliberately dramatic—meant to reflect the cultural self-confidence of an imperial, industrious Glasgow.

Inside, the museum blends fine art, archaeology, natural history, arms and armour, and decorative arts across more than 20 themed galleries. Iconic works include:

- **Salvador Dalí's *Christ of Saint John of the Cross*** (1951), controversial on acquisition, now beloved

- The **Dutch Old Masters** collection, including works by Rembrandt and Van Dyck
- **The Glasgow Boys** and **Scottish Colourists**, chronicling turn-of-the-century artistic rebellion
- Historic displays on **Scotland's wildlife**, **Ancient Egypt**, and **World War history**

But Kelvingrove is also a site of historical contradiction. Many of its artefacts and much of its construction were funded—directly or indirectly—by Glasgow's merchant-elite fortunes, often derived from tobacco, cotton, and sugar trades that relied on colonial exploitation and slavery. In recent years, curators have responded with new interpretation panels that contextualise these legacies.

The museum now emphasises inclusion and accessibility. Community-curated exhibitions, multilingual signage, and outreach programs reflect a commitment to making Kelvingrove a cultural home for *all* Glaswegians, not just those from privileged backgrounds.

2.1.4 The University of Glasgow: Gothic Grandeur and Global Impact

Founded in 1451, the **University of Glasgow** is the fourth-oldest university in the English-speaking world and one of the intellectual cornerstones of the Scottish Enlightenment. Its current hilltop campus at **Gilmorehill**, designed by George Gilbert Scott in the 1870s, is a masterpiece of High Victorian Gothic—its turrets, cloisters, and vaulted arches a striking echo of Oxford and Cambridge. But unlike those southern peers, Glasgow's university has long maintained a robust civic character and working-class accessibility.

Its alumni include:

- **Adam Smith**, philosopher and author of *The Wealth of Nations*, who shaped modern capitalism
- **James Watt**, whose work on steam engines revolutionised global industry
- **Lord Kelvin**, physicist and namesake of the Kelvin temperature scale
- **Joseph Lister**, pioneer of antiseptic surgery
- **Caroline Herschel** and **Isobel Wylie Hutchison**, among the earliest women associated with scientific exploration and study

The university has grown into a global research institution with strengths in medicine, engineering, life sciences, and social policy. Its facilities include:

- **The Hunterian Museum and Art Gallery**, housing anatomical curiosities and the Mackintosh House

- **The Advanced Research Centre (ARC)**, focusing on interdisciplinary innovation
- **The Chapel**, a stunning fusion of faith, memory, and post-war art deco elements

The student population is among the most international in the UK, with over 140 nationalities represented. This global reach is both a strength and a challenge, prompting ongoing conversations about the university's historic wealth (partly linked to the profits of slavery) and its modern mission of justice, inclusion, and decolonisation.

2.1.5 The Slavery Legacy and Ethical Reckoning

In recent decades, academic researchers and activists have begun uncovering and confronting the University of Glasgow's historical links to slavery and colonial wealth. A landmark report published in 2018 revealed that the institution benefited significantly—via bequests, endowments, and trade relations—from individuals whose fortunes were built on the exploitation of enslaved people in the Caribbean and Americas.

In response, the university became the first in the UK to commit to a **"programme of reparative justice"**, including:

- Partnerships with the University of the West Indies
- Scholarships for Caribbean students
- A commitment to further research and transparency

Kelvingrove Museum has also begun auditing its collections for objects acquired during Britain's imperial era, and curators have initiated a public dialogue about restitution and ethical display practices. These measures mark a slow but necessary shift in how Glasgow's elite institutions engage with difficult legacies—placing ethical responsibility alongside educational mission.

2.1.6 The West End and Radical Thought

Despite its associations with affluence and high culture, the area surrounding the university has long been fertile ground for radical politics and progressive social action.

In the late 19th and early 20th centuries, West End lecture halls hosted debates on **women's suffrage**, **Irish independence**, and **Labour reform**. Student activism flourished in response to apartheid, nuclear armament, and war. Feminist collectives and LGBTQ+ organisations began forming here in the 1970s and 1980s, often in resistance to the city's more conservative mainstream.

Mary Barbour, the famed socialist councillor and leader of the 1915 rent strikes, received her education in this environment. More recently, the West End has been a site for climate justice campaigns, anti-racism movements, and creative expressions of dissent—through poetry, art installations, and performance.

Today's University of Glasgow student body reflects this progressive tradition. Initiatives such as the **QMU Debates**, **Glasgow Against Arms Trade**, and **Students of Colour Collective** all carry forward the spirit of critical inquiry and ethical challenge.

2.1.7 Hillhead, Byres Road, and Civic Identity

Surrounding the university are the affluent districts of **Hillhead**, **Dowanhill**, and **Hyndland**, where Victorian and Edwardian sandstone terraces blend with leafy avenues, artisan cafés, and high-end boutiques. The bustling **Byres Road**, once a quiet thoroughfare, now teems with bookstores, patisseries, thrift shops, record stores, and busking musicians.

This area is not just a student haunt—it's a cornerstone of Glasgow's cultural brand. Places like:

- **Ashton Lane** – a cobbled, fairy-lit alley of bars and arthouse cinemas
- **Oran Mór** – a church-turned-venue with murals by Alasdair Gray
- **Òran na Mara** and **Tchai-Ovna** – tea houses with activist flair

The West End Festival, held annually in June, celebrates this blend of tradition and modernity through parades, concerts, open studios, and historical walks. While gentrification and rising rents pose challenges, the area continues to serve as a symbol of Glasgow's intellectual dynamism and cultural pride.

2.1.8 Conclusion: A Tapestry of Influence

Kelvingrove and the University of Glasgow are more than architectural marvels or centres of learning—they are profound expressions of Glasgow's paradoxical identity.

They reveal a city at the crossroads of beauty and brutality, empire and emancipation, privilege and protest.

Here, knowledge was used to justify conquest—and later, to dismantle it. Art was gathered through colonial reach—but now it inspires global dialogue. Wealth was accumulated through exploitation—but today it funds scholarships, research, and repair.

This layered heritage challenges us to understand the past not as a closed chapter, but as a living influence. The West End's spires, galleries, and walkways speak not only to what Glasgow was—but to what it is still becoming: a city where history is not buried but debated, and where learning is inseparable from ethical engagement.

2.2 Ashton Lane and Byres Road: Bohemia and Boutique

2.2.1 Introduction: The Soul of the West End

At the heart of Glasgow's West End lies an enchanting pairing: **Ashton Lane**, a cobbled, whimsical backstreet known for its artsy nightlife, and **Byres Road**, the district's main artery and cultural showcase. Together, they form a microcosm of the West End's charm—an ever-shifting blend of vintage bohemia, student vibrancy, artisanal commerce, and gentrified affluence. These streets reflect both continuity and change: where Glaswegian traditions are preserved, reimagined, and increasingly commercialised.

While often marketed as hip, fashionable, and Insta-worthy, Ashton Lane and Byres Road also possess deeper textures. Here, layers of history reveal a past shaped by middle-class reformers, art-school radicals, and urban developers. This isn't simply a district of cafés and bars; it's a cultural laboratory where heritage and innovation collide.

2.2.2 Byres Road: The West End's Cultural Spine

Stretching roughly from **Great Western Road** at the north down to **Partick Cross** near the River Kelvin, **Byres Road** is the principal commercial corridor of Glasgow's West End. Its importance goes beyond geography: it connects the intellectual nerve centre of the **University of Glasgow** with residential quarters, leisure venues, markets, galleries, and theatres.

Historically, Byres Road was a modest lane through rural fields. Its transformation began in the mid-19th century, when Glasgow's rising middle classes—flush from the Industrial Revolution—sought refuge from the grime and congestion of the city centre. Residential terraces, elegant tenements, and private villas sprang up in Hillhead and Dowanhill, and Byres Road emerged as their communal spine: a place to shop, socialise, and promenade.

Today, the street is a carefully balanced mix of:

- **Boutiques and High-Street Stores**: Independent booksellers, record shops, and thrift stores sit beside chains like Oliver Bonas and Paperchase.
- **Cafés and Bakeries**: Artisan offerings like **Kember & Jones**, **Cottonrake**, and **Twelve Triangles** compete with Costa and Starbucks.
- **International Cuisine**: Reflecting the multicultural makeup of the West End, the street hosts Lebanese, Vietnamese, Indian, and vegan cafés.
- **Vintage and Sustainable Fashion**: Second-hand stores like **Glorious** and **Starry Starry Night** blend retro appeal with sustainability ethics.

Unlike Glasgow's more aggressive commercial zones, Byres Road retains a stroll-friendly rhythm. Locals browse at their leisure, tourists consult guidebooks, students sip flat whites while reading academic journals, and elderly residents catch up over tea. It's a civic space with a distinct tempo—neither hurried nor performative.

2.2.3 Ashton Lane: Cobbled Whimsy with Cultural Depth

Just a few steps off Byres Road lies **Ashton Lane**, one of Glasgow's most iconic and romanticised streets. Its twinkling fairy lights, uneven cobbles, and dense cluster of pubs, eateries, and indie cinemas make it a magnet for visitors and locals alike.

But Ashton Lane wasn't always so curated. In the early 20th century, it was a humble service lane—an inconspicuous alley behind the back entrances of tenements and shops. Its transformation began in the 1970s, largely thanks to artists, architects, and cultural entrepreneurs seeking an alternative to Glasgow's declining city centre.

Pioneering venues like:

- **The Ubiquitous Chip**: Opened in 1971, this was a trailblazing restaurant that defied culinary conventions with seasonal Scottish produce, in contrast to the postwar city's fried-food monotony. Its founder, Ronnie Clydesdale, envisioned it as a place where food, art, and social discourse could flourish. The restaurant is now a multilevel icon, with muraled walls and a rooftop garden.
- **Grosvenor Cinema**: Originally opened in 1921, it was reinvented as an arthouse cinema in the early 2000s. Its plush leather seating, bar service, and independent film programme attract cinephiles across the city.

Ashton Lane has come to symbolise the West End's bohemian spirit. Yet beneath its aesthetic charm lies a complex tension between cultural authenticity and commercial reinvention. Some argue that rising rents and tourism have diluted its original artistic edge, transforming it from an outsider's haven into a gentrified high-end strip.

Still, it remains a beacon for:

- **Intimate gigs and jazz nights**
- **Creative networking meetups**
- **Romantic strolls and pre-theatre drinks**
- **Spontaneous poetry readings and student film festivals**

2.2.4 The Spirit of Bohemia: Intellectualism Meets Hedonism

What gives Ashton Lane and Byres Road their enduring allure is not simply the sum of their cafés, pubs, and boutique shops. It's the ambience of **intellectual bohemia**—a fusion of bookish charm, creative experimentation, and casual rebellion.

This spirit dates back to the late 19th century, when the **Glasgow Art Club**, **University debating societies**, and radical women's circles gathered nearby. Over the 20th century, the area welcomed writers, painters, and political activists disenchanted with the city's more conformist quarters.

Today, that tradition survives through:

- **Live Literature Nights** at the **Hillhead Library**, one of Glasgow's oldest public libraries.

- **Creative Writing Workshops** at **Waterstones Byres Road**, which often hosts debut author launches.
- **Pop-up exhibitions** hosted in former storefronts, blending visual arts with activism.

Young creatives find an atmosphere here that welcomes eccentricity. You'll see it in the way locals dress, the blend of languages on the street, the informal busking jams in lanes, and the hand-illustrated menus at indie cafés. Even as gentrification threatens to sanitise its edges, the West End's creative soul keeps asserting itself.

2.2.5 Coffee, Conversation, and the Third Place

Sociologists speak of the "third place"—not home, not work, but a social environment where people engage informally. Ashton Lane and Byres Road are full of these third places. Cafés like **Kaf**, **Papercup**, and **Eusebi's Deli** are as much about community as caffeine. Tables are strewn with sketchbooks, laptops, open novels, and newspapers. It's not uncommon to overhear a heated philosophical debate beside a quiet Tinder date or freelance Zoom call.

This culture of the third place is crucial to the district's identity. It fosters cross-generational dialogue, creativity, civic involvement, and mental wellbeing. It's also one of the reasons so many graduates from the University of Glasgow stay in the area long after their studies.

2.2.6 Nightlife: Eclectic, Elevated, and Local

By night, the tone shifts. Where Glasgow's city centre clubs often lean toward mainstream energy, the West End's nightlife is more curated, subtle, and story-driven.

Highlights include:

- **Jinty McGuinty's**: A classic Irish pub with a student-friendly vibe, live music, and a packed outdoor patio even in winter.
- **The Belle** and **The Sparkle Horse**: Locally loved bars with deep whisky menus and vintage furniture.
- **Vino Valentino**: An intimate wine bar with organic, biodynamic selections and low-key jazz nights.
- **The Hug and Pint** (nearby on Great Western Road): A hub for underground music and plant-based dining.

Nightlife in this area is more than revelry—it's a continuation of daytime life. Conversations deepen, art ideas are born, and friendships take root.

2.2.7 Gentrification and Cultural Tensions

With its boutiques, Instagrammable spots, and rising rental prices, the West End—especially Ashton Lane and Byres Road—has not escaped the pressures of **gentrification**. Many locals express concern that the district's creative and student-driven essence is being eroded by luxury flats, corporate takeovers, and tourist commodification.

Debates rage over:

- The loss of independent shops
- Studentification vs. residential needs
- Noise complaints vs. nightlife culture
- Corporate homogenisation of once-quirky establishments

Local campaigns have emerged to protect heritage signage, preserve music venues, and cap short-term holiday lets. Ashton Lane in particular stands at the crossroads: beloved but increasingly curated for external consumption.

2.2.8 A Living Canvas of the West End

Despite these tensions, Ashton Lane and Byres Road remain among the most emblematic parts of Glasgow. Their success lies not just in what they offer, but how they **feel**: intimate yet cosmopolitan, traditional yet forward-looking. They are walkable, emotionally resonant, and always slightly unpredictable.

Whether it's a spontaneous ceilidh, a second-hand poetry find, a record-store discovery, or a long-night discussion about politics and art over a dram—this district continues to capture Glasgow's bohemian heart.

2.3 Hillhead and the Lanes: Literary Glasgow and Local Life

2.3.1 Introduction: Hillhead's Quiet Authority

In the heart of Glasgow's storied West End lies **Hillhead**—a neighborhood that balances stately elegance with unassuming intellectual clout. Flanked by bustling **Byres Road**, the charming **lanes**, and steep Kelvin valley slopes, Hillhead may lack the flamboyance of Ashton Lane or the spectacle of Kelvingrove, but it is, in many ways, the soul of the West End: contemplative, layered, and quietly influential.

While tourists may pass through to snap photos or stop for coffee, Hillhead unfolds more slowly for those who linger. Its beauty is not brash but rather curated over centuries: handsome tenement terraces, weathered sandstone walls, narrow passages where poets once wandered, and community hubs still vibrant with Glaswegian character. Hillhead is not merely a residential district—it's an ecosystem of ideas, books, voices, stories, and gardens.

2.3.2 Historical Roots: Victorian Ambitions and the Rise of a Middle-Class Haven

Hillhead's rise parallels Glasgow's transformation during the Industrial Revolution. As the 19th century progressed, the city's merchants, educators, and professionals looked westward, seeking refuge from the soot and noise of the commercial core. Hillhead became their answer.

What was once rural land was systematically shaped into an urban garden suburb. Its development was planned with both elegance and purpose. Townhouses and tenements with expansive bay windows, cast-iron railings, and decorative cornices were constructed with middle-class tastes in mind. Broad avenues like **Great George Street** and **Hillhead Street** were laid out to convey status while remaining intimately scaled for community life.

At its center, **Hillhead Parish Church**, built in 1876, once anchored the neighborhood spiritually. Though no longer serving as a religious institution, it stands today as a historic sentinel of the district's Victorian aspirations. The proximity to the expanding **University of Glasgow**, relocated to nearby Gilmorehill in 1870, ensured Hillhead would always be a magnet for scholars, thinkers, and bookish wanderers.

2.3.3 The Lanes: A Labyrinth of Character and Commerce

Tucked behind and between the more prominent thoroughfares lie the West End's **lanes**—narrow cobbled alleys that define Hillhead's identity. Originally built as service roads for the rear entrances of grand homes and tenements, these lanes have, over time, become urban villages filled with independent businesses, artisan studios, cafés, and quiet residences.

The most notable lanes in Hillhead include:

Cresswell Lane

A charming cluster of boutiques and small eateries, Cresswell Lane is a shopping experience from another era. Here, one might find:

- A locally run vintage clothing store with curated 1960s finds.
- Handcrafted Scottish jewelry made onsite by independent artisans.
- A café tucked behind an antique shop where the menu is written in chalk and the scones are made fresh daily.

Ruthven Lane

More eclectic and less polished than Ashton Lane, Ruthven Lane carries a distinctly bohemian energy. It houses:

- **Voltaire & Rousseau**, perhaps Glasgow's most chaotic and beloved secondhand bookshop. Floor to ceiling piles of books threaten to topple over, with no apparent order except in the mind of the eccentric shopkeeper.
- Quirky thrift stores, offbeat repair shops, and decades-old cafés with mismatched furniture and regulars who've known each other for years.

These lanes resist Glasgow's commercial pressures. Unlike the West End's increasingly gentrified edges, Hillhead's lanes offer **resistance through continuity**. Their charm is not in curated perfection, but in their commitment to localism, individuality, and literary character.

2.3.4 Literary and Academic Life: The Invisible Ink of Hillhead

Hillhead has long been a crucible for Glasgow's literary and intellectual life. Its stone walls have heard the footsteps of professors, poets, radical students, and philosophers. It remains a neighborhood where books and ideas take on architectural form.

Writers and Thinkers

- **Alasdair Gray**, the legendary Glaswegian writer and artist, who called the West End home, frequently roamed Hillhead's streets and imbued its geography into his fiction. His masterpiece, *Lanark*, blends the mundane with the surreal in ways that reflect the West End's own layered character.
- **Liz Lochhead**, former Scots Makar (national poet), often performed in Hillhead's small venues, blending feminist insight, Glaswegian dialect, and classical motifs.

University of Glasgow Influence

Though the campus itself lies just to the west in Gilmorehill, Hillhead's cafés and libraries often act as informal seminar rooms. It's common to find:

- Students rehearsing debates over coffee at **Offshore Café** on Gibson Street.
- Philosophy lecturers holding office hours in the warmth of **The Library at Hillhead**, a modern community building with rooftop views and reading rooms open to all.

- Authors launching books in intimate salons in residents' homes or at cultural spaces like **Hillhead Bookclub**, a restaurant-bar-gallery hybrid that nods to its academic neighbors.

Hillhead isn't just surrounded by literature; it is **saturated** with it.

2.3.5 Residential Character: Tenement Living and Urban Greenery

The Hillhead neighborhood's character is defined in large part by its distinctive **Glasgow tenements**—three-to-four-story residential buildings with bay windows, parquet floors, tiled vestibules, and generous proportions. Unlike modern flats, these homes were designed to be elegant and spacious, catering to middle-class families with aspirations toward dignity and domesticity.

Many tenements have small front gardens or hedgerows, adding to the area's green feel. A walk down **Kersland Street**, **Hyndland Street**, or **Great George Street** is a study in quiet urban grace: sandstone, cherry blossoms in spring, bicycles chained to wrought-iron railings, children's chalk drawings on the pavement, and the occasional fox slipping between bins.

Though gentrification has driven up property values, Hillhead remains **remarkably livable**—walkable, self-contained, safe, and neighborly. Residents range from students and retirees to young professionals and artists, creating an intergenerational blend that fuels civic pride and preserves local traditions.

2.3.6 Community Life: Markets, Festivals, and Everyday Rituals

Hillhead thrives not on spectacle, but on **ritual**—weekly routines that root residents in shared habits and seasonal rhythms.

- **Hillhead Farmers Market** (on Saturdays) brings fresh produce from Ayrshire, local honey, sourdough, handmade soap, and ethical meats. Residents come not only to shop, but to gossip, share recipes, and catch up with stall owners they've known for years.
- **Hillhead Primary School**, one of Glasgow's most diverse and creative primaries, hosts regular community nights and school-wide art exhibitions open to the public.
- **West End Festival**, each June, sees Hillhead's streets filled with open-air concerts, author talks, children's theatre, and pop-up heritage trails.

There's also a dense web of smaller community events:

- **Knitting groups** at local cafés.
- **History walks** led by amateur archivists.
- **Tenant association meetings** posted on notice boards beside independent grocers.

These are the invisible stitches that hold Hillhead together—not glamorous, but vital.

2.3.7 Challenges and Preservation

As with other parts of the West End, Hillhead faces **pressures of change**. Rising rents have made it harder for young creatives and long-standing tenants to remain. Some independent shops have closed, replaced by more commercial operations. Noise complaints from short-term lets have begun to strain relationships.

Local campaigns focus on:

- **Protecting tenement heritage** from overdevelopment.
- **Restricting Airbnbs** to maintain residential integrity.
- **Supporting community-run venues** and ensuring libraries remain open post-austerity.

Despite these pressures, Hillhead's unique cultural and historical DNA has helped it resist wholesale transformation. Its identity is **rooted not just in physical spaces but in collective memory**—of stories told, poems written, and neighbors known by name.

2.3.8 Conclusion: A Quiet Beacon in Glasgow's Literary Landscape

Hillhead is not a neighborhood that shouts. It **whispers**, echoes, and lingers in memory like the closing line of a well-loved novel. Its lanes may be narrow, but they open into whole worlds. Its people may be reserved, but their roots run deep. To know Hillhead is to know a quieter Glasgow—one built on ideas, community, stories, and enduring affection for the simple rituals of urban life.

It's a place to read, to write, to walk, to grow old—**not despite the city, but because of it.**

2.4 Maryhill and the Forth & Clyde Canal: Working-Class Pride and Waterways

2.4.1 Introduction: Maryhill – The Spirit of Grit and Resilience

Maryhill is not merely a district of Glasgow; it is an identity—**fiercely proud, unapologetically working class, historically vital, and culturally rich**. Nestled in the northwestern corridor of the city and defined by the meandering path of the **Forth & Clyde Canal**, Maryhill has long been a community of laborers, tradespeople, and fighters—both literally, in its storied boxing tradition, and metaphorically, in its resistance to gentrification and marginalization.

From the red sandstone tenements lining Maryhill Road to the quiet towpaths of the revitalized canal, this is a place of **industrial legacy and community strength**, where the past is not polished for tourist display but preserved in pub stories, murals, football chants, and the still-standing architecture of a once-thriving manufacturing powerhouse.

Maryhill's soul lies in its **layers**—of hardship, reinvention, local humor, and activism. It's Glasgow's blue-collar heartbeat, and it doesn't skip a beat.

2.4.2 Historical Foundations: From Roman Outpost to Industrial Dynamo

Maryhill's story begins with geography. Situated along the River Kelvin and intersected by the Forth & Clyde Canal, its location made it a natural route for movement, trade, and, ultimately, industrial growth.

- **Roman Roots**: The Romans built **Antonine's Wall**—a northern defensive barrier—through Maryhill in the 2nd century AD. The remains of **Roman forts** and marching camps, especially around the area known as **Summerston**, are a reminder that this corner of Glasgow was strategic long before steel and soot arrived.

- **18th–19th Century Industrial Rise**: The opening of the **Forth & Clyde Canal in 1790** dramatically transformed Maryhill. It connected the River Clyde to the Firth of Forth, creating a trade artery that turned Maryhill into a logistical hub. The canal attracted:

    - **Iron foundries** like the famous **Maryhill Iron Works**
    - **Glassworks**, **timber yards**, **engineering shops**, and **textile mills**
    - **Canal boatmen and lock-keepers**, who settled around the canal in close-knit housing blocks

The area was named after **Mary Hill**, daughter of the Laird of Gairbraid, whose estate was bisected by the canal. Her name endures in every street sign and in the collective memory of the district.

- **Railway and Military Significance**: Maryhill also housed critical infrastructure, such as the **Maryhill Barracks**, built in 1872. These housed British Army regiments and later became temporary housing for refugees and low-income families after decommissioning.

By the late 19th century, Maryhill was a **bustling, working-class district**, drawing people from the Highlands, Ireland, and elsewhere in Glasgow seeking factory and transport jobs. The skyline filled with chimneys, and the soundtrack was one of hammers, steam, and dock cries.

2.4.3 The Forth & Clyde Canal: Artery of Industry and Renewal

The **Forth & Clyde Canal** is both the historical spine and spiritual soul of Maryhill. At once a feat of 18th-century engineering and a 21st-century symbol of regeneration, it weaves through Maryhill's past, present, and future.

Industrial Canal

In its heyday, the canal:

- Transported coal, grain, whisky, timber, and bricks
- Powered Glasgow's manufacturing boom by enabling cheap inland trade
- Employed hundreds as lock operators, barge captains, and dockworkers
- Was lined with warehouses, barge moorings, and mechanical workshops

The canal helped **turn Glasgow into the Second City of the Empire**—and Maryhill was central to that transformation.

Decline and Dereliction

By the mid-20th century, canal transport declined due to road and rail competition. The canal fell into disrepair:

- Locks were blocked or broken
- Water levels were low and stagnant
- Towpaths became overgrown and dangerous
- Industrial buildings were abandoned or demolished

Maryhill, already grappling with deindustrialization, lost one of its major economic lifelines.

Regeneration and Rebirth

Since the 1990s, the Forth & Clyde Canal has undergone a remarkable revival:

- The **Millennium Link Project** (completed in 2001) reopened the canal to navigation for the first time in 35 years
- Towpaths were repaved for cyclists and walkers
- **Canal-side developments** introduced new housing, offices, and green space
- Artistic interventions—sculptures, murals, and floating gardens—celebrate Maryhill's maritime and industrial history

The canal today is a place of **recreation, heritage, and hope**. Locals fish, jog, kayak, and picnic along its banks. Community groups lead cleanups and biodiversity projects. What was once a corridor of commerce is now a **corridor of connection**—linking past and present, urban grit and green renewal.

2.4.4 Built Environment: Tenements, Halls, and Industrial Ghosts

Maryhill's architecture is less polished than the West End's grand avenues but **no less evocative**. It tells stories in brick and stone, soot and soothed stucco.

- **Red and Blonde Sandstone Tenements**: Built between the 1880s and 1920s, these are the backbone of Maryhill's residential grid. Many were built to house canal workers and factory laborers. Though some blocks were demolished during the **post-war clearances**, significant stretches remain, especially along **Maryhill Road**, **Garrioch Road**, and **Shuna Street**.

- **Maryhill Burgh Halls**: One of Maryhill's most iconic buildings, the **Burgh Halls** were constructed in 1878 to serve the then-independent burgh of Maryhill. Featuring:

   - A clock tower and richly carved stone facade
   - **20 stained glass windows** (restored in recent years) depicting trades and industries of the area—an extraordinary visual archive of Maryhill's working class
- **Canal Infrastructure**:

   - The **Maryhill Locks**, a flight of five interconnected canal locks, are a marvel of Georgian-era engineering and still operational.
   - **Lockkeepers Cottages** and **basin-side warehouses**, many converted into cafés, artist studios, and environmental charities
- **Post-war Developments**: Brutalist tower blocks, especially near **Wyndford**, were built to address housing shortages but also symbolized the harsh utilitarianism of urban planning in the 1960s. Today, these towers face an uncertain future amid debates over demolition versus restoration.

2.4.5 Culture, Sport, and Spirit

Maryhill's cultural vitality is not museum-bound—it lives in pubs, football grounds, boxing gyms, and grassroots projects.

Maryhill Football Club

- A proud non-league side, Maryhill FC plays at **Lochburn Park**, an intimate ground with a fiercely loyal following. The club embodies the **DIY spirit of community football**, where the lines between players, fans, and volunteers blur.

Boxing and Community Gyms

- Maryhill is a cradle of Scottish boxing. Generations have trained in gritty gyms with sweat-stained gloves and creaking speedbags. Boxing remains a rite of passage for many young men and women.
- **Clubs like Kelvin ABC and Maryhill Boxing Club** have turned out champions and offered discipline, camaraderie, and escape from hardship.

Street Art and Murals

- Modern Maryhill embraces public art as a way of storytelling. Murals depict local heroes, canal barges, historical trades, and abstract symbols of resilience.
- Underpasses, gable ends, and bridges are canvases for **urban narratives**.

Burgh Halls and Events

- The restored **Maryhill Burgh Halls** now host:
    - Theatre performances
    - Community cinema nights
    - Art exhibitions focused on working-class life
    - Heritage tours and educational workshops

2.4.6 Community Strength and Challenges

Maryhill remains economically challenged, with pockets of deep deprivation—but **its social fabric is tightly woven**.

- **Community Hubs** like **The Maryhill Hub, The Pyramid at Anderston**, and **Maryhill Integration Network** provide support services, cultural programs, and safe spaces.

- **Youth Projects**, such as **Depot Arts** and **Young Maryhill**, engage local teens through music, art, and street outreach.
- **Environmental Justice Initiatives** leverage the canal's revival to connect ecology and equality, especially in climate-impacted areas.

Yet, challenges persist:

- **Poverty and unemployment** still affect many families.
- **Gentrification concerns** arise as development creeps northward from the West End.
- **Public services**—from libraries to GP clinics—have suffered under austerity.

Despite this, Maryhill continues to **organize, protest, volunteer, and adapt**.

2.4.7 Conclusion: Maryhill – Toughness with a Tender Heart

To walk through Maryhill is to **walk through Glasgow's industrial spine**—and to meet a community that refuses to be forgotten. Its proud tenements and lockstones still whisper stories of labor, laughter, and love. The canal flows now with leisure rather than coal, but its waters still reflect the resilience of a people rooted in dignity.

Maryhill isn't glamorous. It's not meant to be. What it offers is something more enduring: **authenticity, struggle, character, and communal pride**. It's the Glasgow that built Glasgow. And it's still building itself—on its own terms.

2.5 Dowanhill and Hyndland: Garden Suburbs and Quiet Power

2.5.1 Introduction: Glasgow's Leafy Enclaves of Prestige

In the heart of Glasgow's West End lies a pair of neighborhoods that whisper rather than shout, where **wealth is worn lightly**, and the rhythm of life slows to a gentle, cultivated tempo. **Dowanhill and Hyndland**, with their tree-lined crescents, Edwardian terraces, and exclusive postcodes, embody a different kind of power—**cultural capital, generational influence, and discreet privilege**.

Unlike the bohemian buzz of Byres Road or the working-class grit of Maryhill, this corner of Glasgow offers **space, symmetry, and serenity**. Yet, beneath its elegance lies a quiet intensity—a neighborhood shaped by **academics, artists, reformers, and professionals** who have long steered the city's political, cultural, and intellectual life.

These are not neighborhoods you stumble into; they're places **passed down, carefully chosen, and fiercely defended**. Welcome to the garden suburbs—where architecture meets aspiration and tradition meets refinement.

2.5.2 Origins and Development: From Country Estates to Urban Prestige

The emergence of Dowanhill and Hyndland as elite residential quarters is a classic story of **urban expansion and aspirational planning**.

- **Dowanhill**:

    ○ Named after **Dowanhill House**, a grand 18th-century country estate once surrounded by orchards and farmland.
    ○ As Glasgow's mercantile and industrial wealth grew in the 19th century, affluent families sought escape from the smoky congestion of the inner city. Dowanhill became one of the earliest examples of **planned suburban living**—close enough to the city for access, but far enough for peace.

- **Hyndland**:
    - Developed more deliberately in the **late 19th and early 20th centuries** as a **garden suburb**, based on enlightened Victorian planning principles.
    - Houses were laid out along curving avenues, crescents, and cul-de-sacs. The focus was on **light, air, greenery, and symmetry**—a counterpoint to the tightly packed tenements and factory smoke of the East End.

Both areas became magnets for **university professors, lawyers, doctors, and intellectuals**, establishing a genteel residential character that endures to this day.

2.5.3 Architectural Identity: Edwardian Grandeur and Urban Harmony

Few neighborhoods in Scotland offer a more cohesive and character-rich residential landscape than Dowanhill and Hyndland. Walking these streets is like moving through an open-air museum of **Edwardian urbanism and Arts & Crafts-inspired domesticity**.

Hyndland's Signature Architecture:

- Hyndland is unique in Glasgow for its **entirely Edwardian streetscape**, developed between 1895 and 1910.

- It is the **only wholly Edwardian conservation area in Scotland**, protected for its uniform character and historical value.
- Buildings are predominantly:
  - **Red sandstone tenements**, but unlike the working-class blocks elsewhere in the city, Hyndland's tenements are **expansive**, with grand stairwells, decorative tiling, and large bay windows.
  - **Four-in-a-block villas** with generous gardens and intricate stonework.
  - Mansions and detached homes on **streets like Kingsborough Gardens and Westbourne Gardens** showcase the height of Edwardian affluence.

Dowanhill's Elegant Diversity:

- Here the architecture is more eclectic:
  - **Victorian villas, Italianate terraces, neo-Gothic row houses**, and **Queen Anne-style homes** sit alongside mid-20th-century infill flats.
  - Streets like **Victoria Crescent Road, Hyndland Road**, and **Highburgh Road** boast beautifully maintained facades, wrought-iron balconies, and landscaped front gardens.
  - Many buildings are now subdivided into flats but retain their original scale and prestige.

Together, these neighborhoods display a **vision of domestic elegance** rooted in principles of beauty, order, and community harmony.

2.5.4 Everyday Life: Quiet Sophistication and Cultured Ease

Living in Dowanhill and Hyndland is a study in **refined urban comfort**. While there are no high streets or bustling commercial hubs within their core, the rhythm of daily life is marked by **artisan cafés, independent grocers, and leafy promenades**.

Local Institutions and Amenities:

- **Hyndland Secondary School** is one of Glasgow's most respected non-denominational schools, attracting families seeking educational excellence.
- **Western Health and Racquets Club** offers tennis, squash, and fitness in genteel surroundings.
- **St Bride's Episcopal Church** on Hyndland Road is a landmark of ecclesiastical Gothic Revival architecture and a hub of community worship.
- **Cuthbertson's Delicatessen, Peckham's**, and independent wine shops stock fine foods and global wines for those with discerning tastes.

Green Spaces:

- **Old Station Park**, a community-managed garden built on a former railway line, offers tranquility in the heart of Hyndland.
- Residents also enjoy easy access to **Botanic Gardens** and **Kelvingrove Park**, only a short stroll away.

This is a neighborhood that values **quiet quality**—where community newsletters matter more than Instagram, and neighbors greet each other with understated warmth.

2.5.5 Literary and Cultural Associations

Dowanhill and Hyndland have long attracted the **creative and intellectual elite** of Glasgow. Their streets have been home to:

- **Alasdair Gray**, the celebrated author and artist, who lived and worked nearby and based many of his surreal, Glaswegian scenes on this part of the city.
- **Muriel Spark**, author of *The Prime of Miss Jean Brodie*, whose experience at **Gillespie's School** (a nearby girls' school) inspired her iconic characters.
- Prominent **professors, musicians, and reformers** associated with the University of Glasgow.

You'll find quiet literary energy in these neighborhoods—in reading groups held in converted church halls, in old libraries with stained glass and carved balustrades, and in bookshops tucked between townhouses.

2.5.6 Preservation and Contemporary Challenges

As one of Glasgow's most desirable residential areas, Dowanhill and Hyndland face ongoing challenges:

- **Property Pressure**: Demand for flats in period buildings has led to rising prices and the slow creep of exclusivity. Younger families and first-time buyers often find themselves priced out.
- **Preservation vs. Modernization**: Conservation rules protect historic architecture but also restrict renovations. Residents must walk a fine line between maintaining heritage and upgrading for modern living.
- **Traffic and Parking**: Narrow residential streets face congestion due to the high density of cars and limited off-street parking—especially near Hyndland railway station.

However, these tensions are managed with active **residents' associations, heritage groups**, and a strong culture of **civic stewardship**.

2.5.7 Conclusion: The Power of Stillness and Stability

Dowanhill and Hyndland are not showy, and they don't need to be. Their charm lies in their **consistency, subtlety, and inherited prestige**. This is Glasgow at its most measured—a world of handwritten school notices, climbing ivy, community fêtes, and polite conversations at the post office.

But don't mistake calm for complacency. These neighborhoods quietly anchor the West End's social, cultural, and intellectual networks. They are places where ideas brew in sunlit studies, where traditions pass through generations, and where civic pride is a matter of quiet duty.

In the story of Glasgow, Dowanhill and Hyndland are the pages where the ink doesn't fade—solid, dignified, and enduring.

Chapter 3: The East – Roots, Resistance, and Renewal

3.1 High Street to Glasgow Cathedral: Origins of a City

3.1.1 Introduction: Where Glasgow Began

Before the glass towers of the financial district, before the steel rails that stretched from Clyde to Calcutta, and before the sandstone crescents of the West End, there was the **High Street**—a narrow spine of stone and cobble that climbs from the River Clyde to a hill crowned by **Glasgow Cathedral**. This is not only the city's **oldest thoroughfare**, but also the **beating origin** of all that Glasgow was, is, and could yet become.

Walking this stretch is like peeling back the layers of a living archaeological site. Every stone tells a story of medieval merchants, monastic devotion, Victorian slum clearance, industrial ambition, civic pride, and twenty-first century regeneration. It is here that **St. Mungo**, Glasgow's patron saint, built his church; where markets bustled beneath timber gables; where a university was founded in the fifteenth century; and where the earliest bones of Glasgow were laid.

This walk is not just a passage through place, but through **time and transformation**—from sacred hill to mercantile might, from decay to renewal.

3.1.2 St. Mungo and the Birth of Glasgow

At the heart of Glasgow's origin story is **St. Kentigern**, more affectionately known as **St. Mungo**, whose missionary work in the sixth century laid the spiritual foundation for the city.

- St. Mungo was said to have been trained at **St. Serf's Monastery** in Fife before traveling west to found a church by the Molendinar Burn—a now-buried stream that once flowed where modern-day **Cathedral Precinct** stands.
- His miracles—immortalized in the city's **coat of arms** (the bird that never flew, the tree that never grew, the bell that never rang, the fish that never swam)—are not just hagiographic folklore but **symbols of Glasgow's identity**.
- A chapel built on the site of his original church grew over centuries into **Glasgow Cathedral**, a beacon of religious authority in Scotland, and an **anchor for the medieval burgh** that emerged around it.

The presence of Mungo transformed this isolated glen into a place of pilgrimage, worship, and settlement. Glasgow's very name is derived from the **Brythonic "Glaschu"**, meaning **"green hollow"**—a fitting moniker for a city born in a river valley and nurtured by monastic care.

3.1.3 Glasgow Cathedral: Stone, Spirit, and Sovereignty

No single building embodies Glasgow's continuity more powerfully than its cathedral. Often overshadowed by more flamboyant cathedrals in Edinburgh or York, **Glasgow Cathedral** (also called **St. Mungo's Cathedral**) is a rare and resilient survivor—a fully intact example of Scottish Gothic architecture from the **medieval era**, untouched by the Reformation's iconoclasm or post-war redevelopment.

Key Features and Historical Significance:

- **Construction** began in the **12th century**, with major additions through the 13th and 15th centuries.
- Built on the site of St. Mungo's original shrine, the crypt beneath the cathedral houses what is believed to be the **saint's tomb**, making it one of the most sacred Christian sites in Scotland.
- The **nave, choir, and central tower** are superb examples of early pointed Gothic style, with ribbed vaults and slender columns offering solemn grandeur rather than baroque extravagance.
- During the Reformation, the building was saved from destruction by the people of Glasgow themselves, who formed a human ring around it, insisting it continue to serve as their parish kirk.
- The cathedral remains **a working church**, affiliated with the **Church of Scotland**, and is a symbol of spiritual endurance across turbulent centuries.

Visitors stepping into its cool, shadowed interior find themselves not merely in a tourist site but in a **repository of centuries**—an edifice of reverence, rebellion, and remembrance.

3.1.4 The Necropolis: City of the Dead, Mirror of the Living

Climbing the hill behind the cathedral, the traveler reaches one of Europe's most hauntingly beautiful cemeteries: **The Glasgow Necropolis**.

- Designed in the Victorian era, inspired by Père Lachaise in Paris, the Necropolis is a garden cemetery for Glasgow's **industrial elite and cultural dignitaries**.
- Over **50,000 individuals** are interred here, though only a fraction have marked graves. The monuments reflect the **ambition, wealth, and Protestant moralism** of nineteenth-century Glasgow—statues of angels, obelisks, and Greco-Roman tombs rising above the city like watchful sentinels.
- The most prominent memorial is to **John Knox**, the Protestant reformer, whose statue looms from the summit—a symbolic guardian over the "second Jerusalem" of Presbyterianism.
- The cemetery is also home to the graves of **architects, shipbuilders, missionaries, and philanthropists**, a testament to Glasgow's role as an imperial powerhouse.

The Necropolis is not merely a resting place, but a panorama of a city's **vanities, virtues, and visions**. From its summit, you see the whole city stretching westward, industrial towers and tenement roofs breaking the skyline like a story still being written.

3.1.5 The High Street: Market Cross to Medieval Campus

Descending from the Cathedral Precinct, the route follows **High Street**, once the **main artery** of the medieval city. It was here that merchants, craftsmen, and monks jostled among horse carts and market stalls, long before Argyle Street or Sauchiehall ever existed.

Highlights of the Medieval and Early Modern High Street:

- **Glasgow Cross** was once the civic heart of the city, where proclamations were read, justice was dispensed, and markets were held. The **Tolbooth Steeple** still stands as a ghost of Glasgow's early civic architecture.
- **Merchant houses**, long since demolished, once lined the High Street, with warehouses, breweries, and workshops giving way to the burgeoning textile and tobacco trades.
- **The University of Glasgow** was originally founded off High Street in 1451, before relocating to Gilmorehill in the 19th century. A **blue plaque trail** now marks the footprint of its original buildings, including the **Old College site** and early lecture halls.

This was the academic and administrative **cradle of the Scottish Enlightenment**, where ideas began to flicker that would go on to influence **economics, medicine, and philosophy** far beyond Scotland.

3.1.6 Victorian Decline and Industrial Displacement

By the 19th century, however, High Street's glory had faded. As wealth and development moved westward, the east of the city—once its heart—became **overcrowded, impoverished, and neglected**.

- **Slum housing** proliferated, with narrow wynds and damp closes packed with workers and laborers drawn by the industrial boom. Disease, deprivation, and squalor marked this phase.
- The area's historic fabric was slowly **erased by tenement clearance, infrastructure projects, and motorway construction**—leaving only fragments of its medieval past clinging to the urban landscape.
- Even the once-sacred **Molendinar Burn** was culverted and buried, hidden beneath asphalt and railway tracks.

Yet, beneath this decay was resilience. **Civic reformers, church missions, and community organizers** sought to reclaim the East End, laying the groundwork for future regeneration.

3.1.7 Renewal and Heritage Revival

In the 21st century, the area surrounding the **High Street and Cathedral Precinct** has undergone a measured revival—balancing **heritage conservation with urban regeneration**.

- The **St. Nicholas Garden and Cathedral Square** have been beautified, offering quiet green respite amid the cityscape.
- The **High Street corridor** has seen the arrival of student housing, arts venues, and entrepreneurial hubs—particularly around **Saltmarket and Trongate**.
- **Community organizations** and the **City Heritage Trust** are actively restoring neglected landmarks and promoting historical literacy among residents and visitors alike.
- Public art installations and heritage trails help tell the story of what was lost—and what endures.

Today, the area is once again attracting **pilgrims of a different sort**—history lovers, architecture buffs, genealogists, and curious walkers—all looking to trace the veins of a city that rose from these very stones.

3.1.8 Conclusion: Walking with the Ancestors

To walk from the Clyde to Glasgow Cathedral is to move **not just uphill, but backward in time**. Here lie the **roots of Glasgow**—sacred, civic, and commercial. The very soul of the city was shaped by this corridor: its spiritual birth, its medieval growth, its industrial pains, and its attempts at rebirth.

Few cities wear their history so openly. Even fewer allow you to walk it in a single mile. But in Glasgow, the path is still here. The stones still whisper. And if you listen closely on the quiet steps of the Necropolis, you might just hear the echoes of Mungo's bell—ringing, still, in the green hollow where it all began.

3.2 Dennistoun and Alexandra Parade: Tenements and Transformation

3.2.1 Introduction: East End Evolution

To truly understand Glasgow, one must venture beyond its postcard landmarks and merchant grandeur. The story of **Dennistoun** and its arterial spine, **Alexandra Parade**, is a tale of **urban planning, working-class dignity, tenement life, and steady reinvention**. It is a district born of Victorian aspiration and shaped by waves of immigration, industry, economic struggle, and community resilience.

Dennistoun is not simply a neighborhood—it is a lens through which to examine the **city's housing legacy**, its cycles of **deprivation and rejuvenation**, and its powerful sense of place. A short walk from the city centre, it has often been overlooked or misunderstood, yet today it stands as one of Glasgow's most **vibrant, diverse, and architecturally fascinating areas**, a proud reflection of East End history and modern-day transformation.

3.2.2 Foundations of a "Respectable Suburb"

Dennistoun's history begins in the mid-19th century, when **Alexander Dennistoun**, a wealthy Glasgow merchant and banker, envisioned a meticulously planned residential district that would offer comfort and respectability to the city's **aspiring middle classes**.

- Between **1861 and the 1890s**, land was acquired and surveyed, and streets were laid out in a **grid pattern**—a modern, hygienic alternative to the cramped wynds of older districts.
- Architect **James Salmon** was hired to design a neighborhood filled with **ornate red and blonde sandstone tenements**, villas, churches, schools, and leafy crescents.
- Dennistoun was intended to rival the grandeur of the West End, minus the aristocratic airs—its tenements were larger and brighter than the slums of the Gorbals or Calton, and boasted architectural flourishes like **turrets, carved lintels, and wrought-iron railings**.

However, the neighborhood's evolution did not strictly follow Alexander Dennistoun's vision. While initially attracting clerks, shopkeepers, and skilled tradespeople, the area soon became a **melting pot of working-class families**, immigrants, and small-business owners drawn by proximity to shipyards, warehouses, and rail depots.

3.2.3 The Rise of the Tenement: Design, Density, and Daily Life

The **tenement** is Glasgow's most iconic residential form—and in Dennistoun, it flourished in both **form and function**.

Tenement Architecture:

- Typical flats comprised a communal **"close"** with four floors, each hosting one or two flats per landing.
- Many featured bay windows, corniced ceilings, recessed alcoves, and original tiled fireplaces—elegant touches even in modest homes.

- Shared **back courts** and drying greens fostered a sense of community among neighbors, who relied on collective responsibility and informal networks for childminding, maintenance, and safety.

Life within the tenements was **social and interconnected**. Front doors were rarely locked, stairwells echoed with children's games and mothers' conversations, and rituals like the weekly "close scrub" helped maintain cleanliness and pride in place. For many, the tenement was more than a dwelling—it was a **social institution**, a crucible of community life.

3.2.4 Alexandra Parade: Artery of Commerce and Connection

Alexandra Parade, named after Queen Alexandra and laid in alignment with the **city's eastern expansion**, has long served as Dennistoun's principal thoroughfare—an axis of **commerce, culture, and change**.

- Running from **Duke Street** in the west toward **Alexandra Park** in the east, the Parade is a showcase of **early 20th-century storefronts**, independent cafes, bakeries, grocers, and more recently, ethnic restaurants and takeaways.
- The **Dennistoun Public Library**, opened in 1905 with funding from Andrew Carnegie, still serves the community—a handsome red sandstone building with civic pride etched into every cornice.
- The street is also home to numerous **educational and medical facilities**, including **Whitehill Secondary School** and the **Glasgow Royal Infirmary's eastern clinics**, making it a hub of local life.
- **Alexandra Parade railway station**, part of the North Clyde Line, links Dennistoun with both city centre and suburban destinations—reinforcing its identity as an accessible, well-connected district.

In the 20th century, the parade underwent numerous changes—some beneficial, others controversial—including phases of dereliction, **urban motorway intrusion**, and piecemeal regeneration. Still, its essence as the commercial and social spine of Dennistoun remains intact.

3.2.5 Industry, Immigration, and Identity

Like much of Glasgow's East End, Dennistoun's identity has been shaped by **waves of industrial labor and immigration**.

- The neighborhood attracted **Irish, Italian, Polish, and Jewish** immigrants from the 19th century onward, many fleeing hardship or persecution and finding both refuge and opportunity in Glasgow.

- Each community left its mark—in churches, delis, synagogues, and in the cultural rhythms of daily life. The **Italian community**, for instance, introduced cafés and ice cream parlors that became beloved features of the area.
- Workers found employment in the vast industrial belt along the Clyde, including **railway yards, foundries, and textile mills**. A significant portion of Dennistoun's population walked daily to their jobs at **Springburn's locomotive works** or the **Parkhead Forge**, home to the massive William Beardmore & Co. steelworks.

In these industries, life was hard—defined by long hours, dangerous conditions, and low pay. But the tight-knit communities that grew in Dennistoun's tenements provided **mutual support networks**, unions, and places of worship that offered dignity amid difficulty.

3.2.6 Alexandra Park: Green Space and Civic Vision

At the eastern end of the district lies **Alexandra Park**, a jewel of **urban Victorian planning** and a key component of Dennistoun's identity.

- Opened in **1870**, the park was designed to bring green relief to the increasingly dense and industrialized East End.
- Its formal layout includes **tree-lined avenues, ornamental gardens, children's play areas**, and a large duck pond.

- The park's most iconic feature is the **Saracen Fountain**, a cast-iron marvel relocated here from Kelvingrove Park after the 1901 International Exhibition.

Alexandra Park has long served as a venue for **family outings, political rallies, summer fêtes, and football matches**, anchoring Dennistoun in both leisure and civic consciousness. In recent years, efforts to maintain and revitalize the park—through community groups, Friends of the Park initiatives, and city council programs—have ensured its continued relevance as a space of **health, heritage, and hope**.

3.2.7 Decline and Renewal: Postwar Change and 21st-Century Revitalization

By the mid-20th century, Dennistoun—like much of inner-city Glasgow—began to suffer from **economic decline and depopulation**.

- The closure of shipyards, steelworks, and tram depots led to rising unemployment and social challenges.
- Some tenements fell into disrepair; others were cleared in favor of low-rise housing or high-rise tower blocks, which often failed to deliver on promises of modernity.
- The construction of the **M8 motorway** carved a deep physical and psychological scar through the community, cutting Dennistoun off from the city centre and altering traffic patterns, air quality, and walkability.

Yet Dennistoun's tenement heart proved **remarkably resilient**. From the 1990s onward, a combination of **heritage-driven restoration, affordable housing demand**, and a growing appreciation for tenement architecture has led to widespread regeneration.

- Today, **new generations of artists, young professionals, students, and migrants** are reshaping Dennistoun's cultural identity.
- Independent coffee shops, vegan cafés, bike repair stores, and bookstores have opened along Duke Street and the Parade.
- **Community arts programs, food banks, co-ops, and social initiatives** have taken root, blending activism with inclusivity.
- In 2020, *The Times* controversially listed Dennistoun as one of the **"coolest neighborhoods in the UK"**, sparking both pride and skepticism from locals wary of gentrification.

Still, the essence of Dennistoun remains: a **working-class neighborhood with a strong backbone**, proud of its roots, its resilience, and its refusal to be neatly defined.

3.2.8 Conclusion: Between Memory and Momentum

Dennistoun and Alexandra Parade are places of continuity and contradiction. Here, **nineteenth-century tenements** line streets filled with **Pakistani grocers, Polish bakeries, and Scottish chip shops**. Young families picnic in parks planted by Victorians. Students sip artisan coffee in buildings where dockworkers once laid their boots.

This district tells a story of **urban design and community defense**, of **immigration and invention**, of **challenge and renewal**. It is a living chapter in the saga of Glasgow—one where transformation has not erased memory, but enriched it.

To walk through Dennistoun is to walk through **layers of lived experience**—a tenemented terrain that continues to teach Glasgow how to adapt, resist, and grow.

3.3 The Barras, Calton, and Glasgow Green: Markets, Music, and Memory

3.3.1 Introduction: The East End's Beating Heart

To encounter the **soul of Glasgow**, one must spend time not only in its architectural showpieces or genteel districts, but in the **raw, layered spaces of the East End**—where **commerce, protest, music, and memory** collide in cobbled lanes and red-bricked markets. This is the realm of **The Barras**, **Calton**, and **Glasgow Green**—a triad that has long defined Glasgow's **working-class culture**, its resistance to authority, its musical creativity, and its passion for public life.

These areas are not mere relics of the past. Though shaped by the **industrial revolution**, **immigration**, and the **pressures of modern urban life**, they remain vital spaces of **East End identity**—where **tradition and reinvention**, **grit and grace**, exist in dynamic tension. Together, they form a richly textured stage on which the dramas of city life—public assembly, economic struggle, street performance, and social protest—have played out for centuries.

3.3.2 The Barras: Market Culture and Working-Class Enterprise

No part of Glasgow better encapsulates the **spirit of enterprise, patter, and resilience** than the **Barras Market**—short for "barrows," the carts once used by vendors to hawk their goods.

Origins and Growth:

- The Barras began in the **1920s**, when **Maggie McIver**, a market entrepreneur of formidable determination, responded to the chaotic street-trading culture of Calton by creating a covered market space where working-class traders could rent barrows and stalls.
- Initially held outdoors in Calton's narrow streets, the Barras soon expanded into **roofed arcades**, warehouses, and walled courtyards filled with stalls selling everything from **linoleum and lamps to suits, records, china, tools, and toys**.

Atmosphere and Commerce:

- On weekends, the Barras came alive with a **cacophony of banter**, sales pitches, music, and conversation—"Get yer deals here!" echoing between buildings.

- Vendors were known for their **sharp wit, improvisational selling techniques**, and capacity to **entertain as much as sell**. Shopping was never a sterile transaction—it was theatre.
- Visitors would browse **second-hand treasures**, **dubious electronics**, **knock-off clothing**, and **Glasgow Rangers or Celtic memorabilia**, while grabbing food from fish-and-chip vans or tea rooms tucked between the stalls.

For decades, the Barras functioned as an **alternative high street** for working-class Glaswegians. It offered **affordable goods, informal credit, social connections**, and a rich oral culture of storytelling and negotiation. To shop at the Barras was to be immersed in the rhythms and cadences of **East End life**, where commerce and community were inseparable.

3.3.3 The Barrowland Ballroom: Music, Memory, and Iconic Sound

Attached to the market is the **Barrowland Ballroom**, a sacred site in Glasgow's musical history and one of the most beloved concert venues in the UK.

From Dancehall to Legend:

- Opened in **1934** by Maggie McIver herself, the Barrowland Ballroom was initially a **dance venue** intended for market workers and traders to unwind. It combined **a sprung maple dancefloor**, neon-lit signage, and a capacity for over a thousand dancers.
- Destroyed by fire in 1958 and rebuilt in 1960, the new building became a legend in its own right. Its glittering ceiling, **retro signage**, and gritty vibe attracted generations of Glaswegians.

Musical Rebirth:

- From the **1970s onward**, the Barrowlands shifted from dancehall to **rock and alternative concert venue**, hosting iconic performances by **David Bowie, The Clash, Simple Minds, Oasis, U2**, and countless others.
- It became known not only for its **exceptional acoustics** but for the **intensity of the Glasgow crowd**—passionate, unfiltered, deeply knowledgeable.

To this day, playing "the Barras" is a **rite of passage** for bands, a stamp of credibility and connection with the city's musical roots. For fans, it's a place where **memories are made, emotions run high**, and **the ghosts of Glasgow's music past** seem to echo between every note.

3.3.4 Calton: Struggles, Song, and Solidarity

Immediately west of the Barras lies **Calton**, a district with a reputation that belies its rich and complex history. Often synonymous with poverty or sectarianism in public imagination, Calton is in fact one of **Glasgow's oldest and most historic neighborhoods**—a place of **craftsmen, weavers, radicalism**, and **enduring community ties**.

The Calton Weavers and Labour Struggles:

- Calton was once home to a thriving community of **handloom weavers**, artisans whose skill and independence made them both proud and politically aware.
- In **1787**, these weavers staged what became one of the earliest labour strikes in Britain, demanding higher wages and better conditions. The government responded with **military force**—three weavers were killed and several wounded in what became known as the **Calton Weavers' Massacre**.
- A memorial in **Abercromby Street Cemetery**, with the names of the fallen weavers, stands as a **powerful monument to early labour activism** in Scotland.

Sectarian Divides and Community Spirit:

- In the 19th and early 20th centuries, Calton became a densely populated area with significant **Irish Catholic immigration**, which contributed to the entrenched **sectarian divide** between Protestant and Catholic communities.
- However, despite these tensions, Calton has long been defined by a **robust local identity**, fiercely loyal to its own and protective of its institutions, including parish churches, schools, and pubs.
- Street football, community halls, youth clubs, and bands formed the fabric of daily life. Generations of families have lived in the same tenements, preserving **intergenerational ties** even through economic hardship.

Today, Calton is undergoing slow change, with new housing, social initiatives, and arts organizations taking root—though concerns about **gentrification and displacement** continue to animate local ddebates

3.3.5 Glasgow Green: Protest, Recreation, and Public Life

Glasgow Green, the city's oldest public park, lies just south of the Barras and Calton—an expansive green space that has served as **lungs, stage, and soapbox** for the people of Glasgow since the 15th century.

Historical Significance:

- First granted to the people of Glasgow by **Bishop Turnbull in 1450**, Glasgow Green has long been a site of **public gathering, social protest, and leisure**.
- In the 18th and 19th centuries, it was a meeting point for **Chartists, trade unionists, and suffragettes**—a fertile ground for radical politics and collective action.
- Major events such as the **Battle of the Green**, the **1919 strike marches**, and more recently, anti-Iraq War and climate change protests, have continued this tradition of **public expression and democratic vitality**.

Civic Features:

- The **People's Palace**, built in 1898, is a museum dedicated to the **social history of Glasgow**—a working-class response to the high culture of Kelvingrove. It documents tenement life, strikes, holidays at the seaside, and household traditions.
- Adjacent lies the **Winter Gardens**, a Victorian-era glasshouse filled with subtropical plants and a sanctuary from the city's weather.
- **Nelson's Monument**, the **Doulton Fountain** (the world's largest terracotta fountain), and various war memorials add layers of imperial and civic history to the landscape.

Green Space for the People:

- For centuries, the Green has been where Glaswegians **walk their dogs, play football, ride bikes, host barbecues**, or simply **gather to talk and breathe**.
- It has hosted everything from **mass protests and music festivals** (such as TRNSMT and Radio 1's Big Weekend) to quiet moments of reflection.
- Its location, bridging east and central Glasgow, makes it a literal and symbolic **common ground**—a democratic space in a city often divided by class and postcode.

3.3.6 Resilience and Renewal: The East End Today

Today, the areas of the **Barras, Calton, and Glasgow Green** are undergoing a slow but **contested revival**.

- Independent galleries, creative hubs, music studios, and **street art collectives** have taken over old warehouses and shops.
- Initiatives like **Barras Art and Design (BAaD)** and the **Wasps Studios** offer platforms for local artists and host events blending music, fashion, and food.

- The 2014 Commonwealth Games brought new attention to the East End's infrastructure and legacy, but also fueled concerns about **cultural erasure and gentrification**.

Still, the East End continues to produce and protect its own. The **Barras remains open**, if smaller than before. The **Ballroom still sells out**. Calton's murals now commemorate both its past and future. Glasgow Green is still where you go to speak, to breathe, to be heard.

3.3.7 Conclusion: Songlines of the East

From the **buzz of a Saturday market** to the **thunder of a concert drumbeat**, from the **chant of a protest** to the **quiet rustle of leaves in Glasgow Green**, this part of the city tells its story through **sound, memory, and endurance**.

The Barras, Calton, and Glasgow Green are not just locations—they are **living archives of Glasgow's collective soul**. They represent the **intersection of protest and play**, of **commerce and compassion**, of **history and heart**. In every cobblestone and close, every gate and graffitied wall, Glasgow speaks in a voice shaped by its people—raw, witty, proud, and defiantly alive.

Certainly! Here's **Chapter 3.4: Duke Street to Parkhead: Football, Faith, and Factories**, written in your preferred **detailed, comprehensive, and bulky** format, following the established narrative tone and structure:

3.4 Duke Street to Parkhead: Football, Faith, and Factories

3.4.1 Introduction: The Arteries of East Glasgow

From the long, linear stretch of **Duke Street**—one of Glasgow's most historic and industrious thoroughfares—to the legendary **Parkhead district**, where faith and football intermingle with memory and manufacturing, this corner of the East End pulses with the echoes of **working-class resilience, cultural identity**, and **collective pride**.

Once lined with **factories, schools, foundries**, and **tenement housing**, and now partly reimagined through regeneration projects and sports infrastructure, this part of Glasgow remains rooted in a deep **sense of place and belonging**. Here, grand narratives—of **Catholic immigration, football glory**, and **industrial might**—unfold at the street level in **chapels, stadiums, schools**, and **stone-walled ruins**.

This stretch is not merely a geographical corridor—it is a **social artery**, shaped by sweat, steel, worship, and weekend matches. From the **clanging of machinery** to the **chants of the terraces**, the landscape tells the story of a city defined by **labour and loyalty**.

3.4.2 Duke Street: Scotland's Longest Street and Industrial Backbone

Duke Street, stretching from the edge of the city centre at High Street eastward toward Parkhead, is said to be the **longest street in Scotland**. But more than its physical length, it is the density of its **social and industrial history** that marks it as one of Glasgow's most important avenues.

Institutions and Industry:

- Historically, Duke Street was home to some of Glasgow's most notable **factories and institutions**, including the **Duke Street Women's Prison**—an austere red sandstone structure that housed women from the late 19th century until 1955.
- Further along was **John and William Fullarton's chemical works**, the **McLennan rubber factory**, and the **Dennistoun Flour Mill**—all reminders of the street's industrial diversity.

- During the **late 19th and early 20th centuries**, the street boomed with **shopfronts, pubs, cinemas**, and **workshops**, making it a buzzing centre of East End daily life.

The People's Street:

- Tenements rose up beside ironworks; **grocers stood adjacent to garment workshops**. Children played in closes and pend stairways while their parents laboured in factories or queued at coal shops.
- The street was an artery not just of commerce, but of **community interaction**, linking families, parishes, and neighbourhoods.
- In the post-war era, the street faced periods of **decline**, but pockets of resilience remained—particularly through **locally owned businesses, community halls**, and **faith institutions** that kept the area socially intact.

Today, though some factories have disappeared and gentrification nibbles at the edges, Duke Street remains a **key historic spine** of the East End's urban identity.

3.4.3 Faith and Migration: The Catholic East End

The East End, and particularly the areas from Duke Street to Parkhead, were deeply shaped by **waves of Irish immigration** in the 19th and early 20th centuries. For many, faith and community were intertwined—and **Catholicism** became not only a spiritual home, but a **shield and anchor** in a hostile, sectarian environment.

Irish Immigration and Parish Life:

- Fleeing famine, persecution, and poverty, **Irish Catholic migrants** arrived in huge numbers from the mid-1800s, many settling in the tenement districts of Glasgow's East End where industrial jobs were plentiful.
- Parishes like **St. Mary's, Sacred Heart**, and later **St. Michael's** and **St. Anne's** became centres of **worship, education, and identity**.
- **Catholic schools**, supported by parish networks, offered a pathway toward social mobility and stability for generations of East End children.

Sectarian Division:

- This part of Glasgow was long defined by **sectarian fault lines**, often expressed through football allegiances, political ideologies, and social institutions.
- Orange Walks and Catholic processions, though representing different traditions, often shared space—sometimes peacefully, sometimes not—on these same streets.

- Despite episodes of violence and exclusion, Catholic communities in the East End forged strong institutions, cultural networks, and resilient civic identities.

3.4.4 Parkhead: A Stadium, a Symbol, a Community

At the eastern end of Duke Street rises one of Glasgow's most iconic structures: **Celtic Park**, commonly referred to as **Parkhead**. But the stadium is more than bricks and turf—it is the **beating heart of a global fanbase**, the **anchor of a working-class neighbourhood**, and a **symbol of Catholic and Irish-Scottish pride**.

The Birth of Celtic:

- **Celtic Football Club** was founded in **1887** by **Brother Walfrid**, a Marist Brother and Irish Catholic, with the explicit mission of alleviating poverty in the East End through sport.
- The club's roots in **faith, charity, and the Irish diaspora** gave it a unique identity, contrasting with Rangers' Protestant and unionist leanings.
- Parkhead became home to Celtic in **1892**, and the stadium was rebuilt and modernised throughout the 20th century into the 60,000-seat arena seen today.

Community and Belonging:

- For local residents, Celtic is more than a team—it is **a cultural institution, a social identity**, and a **repository of memory**. Matchdays bring life to pubs, chippies, and merchandise stalls.
- Supporters' clubs, song traditions, and commemorative murals throughout the East End—featuring figures like **Tommy Burns**, **Jock Stein**, and **Brother Walfrid**—testify to the profound emotional landscape surrounding the team.
- The club has also been involved in **local charitable efforts**, including through the **Celtic Foundation**, further intertwining its identity with the social fabric of the area.

Parkhead is a physical space, yes, but also a **mental and emotional home** for Glaswegians across generations.

3.4.5 Factories and Foundries: Labour in the East End

While faith and football are powerful forces here, they stand alongside the older story of **labour**—of men and women who worked in the **mills, forges, breweries, and foundries** that lined these streets.

Steel and Engineering:

- The **Parkhead Forge**, one of Glasgow's largest iron and steelworks, dominated the industrial skyline for over a century. It opened in the **late 19th century** and expanded rapidly during the wars to supply munitions, ship parts, and rail equipment.
- Generations of workers toiled in brutal conditions, but the Forge also offered steady employment and a sense of **collective pride**. It had its own **workers' union hall, football team**, and **welfare schemes**.

The Decline of Industry:

- The 1970s and 1980s saw the collapse of traditional industries. Like other parts of the East End, Parkhead and Duke Street faced **unemployment, urban decay**, and social dislocation.
- The Forge closed in **1983**, and while part of the site was eventually redeveloped into **The Forge Shopping Centre**, the loss of skilled industrial work was profound.

Even so, **fragments of this industrial world** remain—faded signs, redbrick shells, and stories passed down from fathers to sons. These remnants keep the past alive amidst the flux of modern transformation.

3.4.6 Present and Future: Change, Challenge, and Identity

Today, the corridor from **Duke Street to Parkhead** is in a **state of transition**. Efforts at **urban regeneration**, often tied to the legacy of the 2014 Commonwealth Games, have brought new housing, roads, and sporting infrastructure—but not always without controversy.

- **New housing developments** have replaced some crumbling tenements, but also raised questions about affordability and local displacement.
- Local schools, churches, and clubs continue to provide **social cohesion**, but funding pressures and political neglect are persistent concerns.
- Yet the presence of **Celtic Park**, community festivals, faith groups, and long-standing family ties keeps the area anchored to its **roots and traditions**.

The East End—like Glasgow itself—is caught between **post-industrial memory and present-day reinvention**. The identity here is complex: one foot in the past, another facing forward. It's a district shaped by **football chants, factory whistles, church bells, and street voices**, all echoing in the same urban soundscape.

3.4.7 Conclusion: Where Labour, Loyalty, and Legacy Converge

Duke Street to Parkhead is more than a route—it is a living **document of Glasgow's working-class experience**. Here, the **factory whistle meets the church hymn**, the **match-day roar meets the quiet dignity of parish life**, and the **industrial ruin shares space with new beginnings**.

It is a part of the city where **football is religion, faith is heritage**, and **labour is legend**. The people who lived, worked, prayed, and played here have left an imprint not only on the built environment but on Glasgow's cultural DNA.

In the weathered brick of a tenement wall, the bronze of a statue outside Parkhead, the hush of an empty chapel, or the smile of a lifelong supporter in a green-and-white scarf—you'll find the truth of this place. A truth forged in steel, strengthened by community, and sustained by memory.

3.5 Bridgeton and Dalmarnock: Sport, Steel, and Survival

3.5.1 Introduction: Two Neighbourhoods, One Heartbeat

Bridgeton and Dalmarnock lie in the inner East End of Glasgow, nestled between **Glasgow Green, Parkhead, and Rutherglen**. Though distinct in geography and identity, these two communities share **a legacy of heavy industry, resilient**

working-class spirit, and deep social bonds forged through generations of labour, migration, and cultural struggle.

Historically central to Glasgow's **engineering and manufacturing might**, the area around Bridgeton Cross and the Clyde-side mills of Dalmarnock once echoed with the clang of metal presses and the footfall of thousands of workers pouring out of vast factories at shift's end. Over time, these neighbourhoods became **centres of political activism, tenement life, boxing gyms**, and **tight-knit community networks** that weathered everything from war to urban neglect.

In the 21st century, Dalmarnock in particular became a focal point for **urban renewal**, culminating in its role as a host site during the **2014 Commonwealth Games**. But behind the glassy facades of new flats and sports arenas lies a story of **loss, hope, endurance**, and the ever-tense balance between regeneration and gentrification. To walk the streets of Bridgeton and Dalmarnock is to trace **Glasgow's post-industrial soul**—scarred but unbroken.

3.5.2 Bridgeton: A Political and Cultural Powerhouse

Bridgeton—or "The Brigton," as locals call it—has long been **a bastion of political engagement, trade unionism, and community pride**. Centered on the busy hub of **Bridgeton Cross**, this neighbourhood's grid of red sandstone tenements and civic buildings tells the story of a community shaped as much by **collective action** as by industrial labour.

Bridgeton Cross and Civic Architecture:

- The six-road junction at **Bridgeton Cross** is anchored by the **Bridgeton Umbrella**, a cast-iron Victorian shelter originally built in **1875** and restored in the early 21st century. It remains an iconic symbol of the district and a common meeting point for residents.

- The **Bridgeton Library**, designed by architect James Robert Rhind and opened in **1906**, is one of Glasgow's Carnegie-funded libraries—a beacon of working-class education and self-improvement.

The Labour Tradition:

- Bridgeton has deep roots in **labour movements and socialist politics**. It was a stronghold of the **Independent Labour Party** in the early 20th century and later played a key role in Glasgow's **Red Clydeside** era, when mass protests and strikes swept the city.
- Activists such as **James Maxton**, **John Wheatley**, and later **Jimmy Reid** and others found a politically fertile home in Bridgeton. It was also home to the **Bridgeton and Calton Co-operative Society**, promoting mutual aid and fair access to food and goods.

Sport and Spirit:

- Bridgeton also carved out a name for itself in **amateur boxing**, with clubs like **Bridgeton Boys' Club** producing champions and offering discipline and solidarity in a tough environment.
- In sport, music, and grassroots politics, Bridgeton sustained itself through **community resilience**, even as industry fell away and public investment waned.

Today, efforts by organisations such as the **Bridgeton Community Learning Campus** and **People's Palace outreach groups** seek to preserve and reinvigorate the district's rich cultural legacy.

3.5.3 Dalmarnock: From Iron and Gas to Games and Gentrification

Dalmarnock, lying just south of Bridgeton along the River Clyde, was once a vital cog in Glasgow's **industrial machine**. The area was home to **gasworks, textile mills, power stations**, and a tangle of railway depots and bridges. Its close proximity to the river and rail made it an ideal site for heavy industry, but also made it vulnerable to economic decline when that industry collapsed.

The Industrial Age:

- The **Dalmarnock Gasworks**, opened in the 19th century, was one of the largest in Scotland. Its towering gasometers dominated the skyline and its distribution network heated and lit vast swathes of Glasgow.

- Mills and engineering works filled the area. Families lived in **tenement rows built beside chimneys and furnaces**, breathing in the by-products of the same industry that paid their wages.
- Despite the grime, Dalmarnock was once a thriving community. People shopped at **local butchers and co-ops**, attended school, and lived within walking distance of extended family and workplaces.

The Long Decline:

- In the **1970s and 1980s**, deindustrialisation hit Dalmarnock hard. As plants shut down and jobs vanished, so did many of the people. A once-busy neighbourhood became marked by **demolition, dereliction**, and **social neglect**.
- The area saw a dramatic **population collapse**, and many of the remaining residents faced **poverty, underinvestment**, and housing decay. What remained was often a shell of the once-thriving community.

3.5.4 The 2014 Commonwealth Games: Regeneration or Displacement?

In the early 2000s, Dalmarnock found itself at the centre of an ambitious redevelopment project tied to **Glasgow's successful bid to host the 2014**

Commonwealth Games. Planners promised **revitalisation, opportunity**, and **economic renewal**—but the results have been mixed and deeply contested.

The Games Village:

- The **Athletes' Village**, built on former industrial land and cleared housing plots, brought sleek, eco-friendly homes and streetscape improvements. After the Games, it was converted into a new residential area with hundreds of housing units.
- The nearby **Emirates Arena** and **Sir Chris Hoy Velodrome**, cutting-edge facilities used during the Games, brought international attention to a long-overlooked district.

Community Impact:

- While some welcomed the new infrastructure and investment, many residents were **displaced through compulsory purchase orders**, and the promises of long-term jobs and affordability did not always materialise.
- Long-standing families and neighbourhoods were **fragmented**, and critics have pointed to the **erasure of Dalmarnock's industrial heritage** in favour of sterile, corporate-style development.

The Legacy:

- Today, Dalmarnock is a neighbourhood in transition—**cleaner, quieter, and greener** than before, but arguably less connected to its past. Local activists continue to push for **community ownership**, affordable housing, and **sustainable regeneration** that includes—not displaces—its people.

3.5.5 The River Clyde: A Lifeline and a Border

The River Clyde runs along the southern edge of Dalmarnock and has long served as **both a life-giving artery and a psychological border**. In the 19th and early 20th centuries, it was a waterway of commerce and a gateway for shipbuilding and transport. Today, it is at the heart of **urban renewal strategies** and environmental projects.

- The **Dalmarnock Bridge**, linking the area to Rutherglen, has stood since **1891**—a key crossing point for workers and families over the decades.
- Efforts to **reclaim the Clyde's banks** as green space, cycle routes, and community gardens aim to reconnect residents with the river that once sustained their industries.

The Clyde is more than a body of water—it is a **symbol of Glasgow's transition**, from a city of coal and smoke to one of bikes, walking trails, and regeneration debates.

3.5.6 Resilience, Memory, and the East End Future

What binds Bridgeton and Dalmarnock together is a shared narrative of **hardship, adaptation, and community tenacity**. These neighbourhoods have endured poverty, political neglect, and erasure—but they have also produced **fighters, scholars, artists**, and **activists**.

Memory and Identity:

- Local archives, oral history projects, and murals around Bridgeton Cross and Dalmarnock Bridge keep memory alive. The stories of **tenement life**, of **boxers and trade unionists**, of **furnacemen and footballers**, still reverberate through the voices of older residents.
- Murals such as those by **Art Pistol Projects** and **local youth groups** honour the legacy of those who fought for rights, recognition, and respect.

The Way Forward:

- Community centres, boxing clubs, libraries, and grassroots campaigns continue to nurture the next generation. There is increasing awareness that **regeneration must be done with—not to—communities**.
- A new chapter is being written in Dalmarnock and Bridgeton—one that mixes **hope with caution**, and **development with heritage protection**.

3.5.7 Conclusion: Grit, Glory, and Glasgow's Heartbeat

Bridgeton and Dalmarnock are not tourist districts, and they don't often feature in glossy guidebooks—but to understand Glasgow's true story, you must walk their streets. Here, between **boxing gyms and glassy sports arenas, abandoned rail depots and new cycle paths**, lies the story of a city that has been **broken and rebuilt**, again and again.

It is the story of **labourers and local legends**, of **steel and survival**, of **community halls and Commonwealth arenas**. And it is not finished yet.

3.6 Tollcross and Shettleston: Garden Suburbs, Swimming Pools, and Working-Class Pride

3.6.1 Introduction: Glasgow's Eastern Resilience and Renewal

Tollcross and Shettleston, nestled deep in the **East End of Glasgow**, represent two of the city's most emblematic post-industrial communities. They sit to the east of Dalmarnock and Parkhead, forming a part of the broader Clyde-side spine of once-thriving working-class neighbourhoods. Their histories are tied closely to the evolution of **municipal housing, railway expansion, coal mining**, and **iron production**, but also to the shifting ideologies of **public health, urban planning**, and **civic well-being**.

While not typically high on tourist itineraries, these neighbourhoods hold a vital place in Glasgow's social and cultural memory. From the **Tollcross International Swimming Centre**, a legacy of the Commonwealth Games, to **Shettleston's red sandstone terraces**, vibrant football culture, and community-led sustainability initiatives, this area remains a proud symbol of working-class pride, strength, and adaptation.

Together, Tollcross and Shettleston embody the **gritty backbone** of the East—neighbourhoods that wear their struggles openly but continue to evolve through the **actions of engaged locals**, **grassroots activism**, and **slow-burn regeneration** efforts that aim to preserve their soul.

3.6.2 Tollcross: Parks, Pools, and Public Good

Tollcross was historically a village on the outskirts of Glasgow, eventually absorbed into the city as industrial expansion moved eastward. It has retained a **green and open feel** due to the presence of **Tollcross Park**, yet it remains quintessentially Glaswegian in its architecture, spirit, and grit.

Tollcross Park and Winter Gardens:

- **Tollcross Park**, one of the most beautiful public green spaces in the East End, was gifted to the city by the Dunlop family in the late 19th century. It is known for its **formal gardens, tree-lined walks**, and the magnificent **Tollcross Winter Gardens**, a vast Victorian glasshouse.
- Though damaged and now awaiting restoration, the Winter Gardens are a reminder of the **municipal pride and investment in green space** that marked Glasgow's emergence as a modern city in the 19th and 20th centuries.

The International Swimming Centre:

- The **Tollcross International Swimming Centre** is one of the East End's most significant recent redevelopments. Renovated and expanded for the **2014 Commonwealth Games**, it features a **50-metre Olympic-standard pool**, used by international teams and local clubs alike.
- It is both a professional venue and a community facility, offering a rare space where elite sport and local access are genuinely intertwined—a beacon of **inclusive public sport**.

Community and Culture:

- Tollcross has a long-standing **loyalism and unionist culture**, visible in the murals, flags, and local lodges. While this political identity remains strong, the community is far more diverse than stereotypes suggest.
- Projects such as **Tollcross YMCA, Eastbank Community Hub**, and **local school collaborations** offer educational support, youth engagement, and health resources in an area still facing significant challenges related to poverty and addiction.

3.6.3 Shettleston: Red Sandstone and Reinvention

Shettleston, just east of Tollcross, is a district defined by both its **tenement tradition** and its **desire to reclaim and reimagine its future**. Once a coal-mining and railway hub, Shettleston's fortunes have risen and fallen in tandem with Glasgow's wider economic shifts—but its streets, people, and culture remain deeply proud and rooted.

Industrial Past:

- The arrival of the **railway in the mid-19th century** transformed Shettleston from a quiet village into a booming suburb. Rows of red sandstone tenements and workers' cottages were built to house the influx of railway employees, factory labourers, and miners.
- The area became home to a wide array of trades, and the **Shettleston railway yards**—though long gone—were once among the busiest in the East End.

Urban Renewal and Housing:

- Like many East End neighbourhoods, Shettleston was heavily affected by **deindustrialisation**, poor housing stock, and socio-economic deprivation from the 1970s onward.
- However, the **Shettleston Housing Association**, founded in 1976, has become a national leader in **sustainable urban housing and community**

empowerment. It has spearheaded renovation projects that blend heritage preservation with eco-conscious design, including **solar-powered homes**, **retrofits of Victorian buildings**, and **intergenerational housing schemes**.
- These developments represent some of the most ambitious examples of **community-led regeneration** anywhere in Scotland, combining **environmental justice**, **social care**, and **heritage**.

Green Initiatives and Food Justice:

- **Shettleston Growing Project**, launched by residents and supported by local authorities, encourages **community gardening**, sustainable food production, and ecological education. It reflects a growing movement toward **self-sufficiency and food security** in post-industrial communities.
- The area has embraced **urban beekeeping, composting**, and **reclaimed land use**, turning former derelict plots into spaces of productivity and healing.

3.6.4 Faith, Football, and Identity

Faith and Religious Diversity:

- Tollcross and Shettleston have traditionally been **Christian-majority areas**, with Protestant churches dominating the religious landscape. However, recent demographic changes have brought greater diversity, including **Eastern European Catholic congregations** and growing numbers of secular residents.
- Churches continue to play a key role in providing **social services, food banks, community kitchens,** and safe spaces, especially for older residents and those facing hardship.

Football and Local Loyalty:

- The area's proximity to **Celtic Park** in nearby Parkhead guarantees a strong presence of Celtic supporters, but local football allegiances also include small amateur and youth teams such as **Eastbank Boys Club** and **Shettleston Juniors**, who play at **Greenfield Park**.
- Football here is more than a pastime—it's a **vehicle for identity, belonging, and aspiration**. Many families pass down club affiliations through generations, and local parks buzz with weekend matches, shouts of encouragement, and grassroots coaching.

3.6.5 East End Challenges and Local Strengths

Tollcross and Shettleston continue to face many of the same socio-economic challenges that affect post-industrial neighbourhoods across the UK:

- **Health inequalities**, particularly around life expectancy and addiction
- **Food insecurity** and reliance on food banks
- **Low employment opportunities** and under-resourced public transport
- **Stigmatization**, both within Glasgow and nationally

Yet, what defines these areas most is not deprivation, but **resilience and regeneration** driven by community effort.

- Locals have championed initiatives to combat **fuel poverty**, increase **green infrastructure**, and protect **affordable housing**.
- Youth programs offer alternatives to gang culture and support educational achievement.
- Projects like **East End Flat Pack Meals** and **Zero Waste Scotland's outreach in Shettleston** empower residents through shared skills and sustainable practices.

3.6.6 Conclusion: A Tale of Two Districts, One Unfolding Future

Tollcross and Shettleston are places of history, hardship, and heart. From **Victorian glasshouses and world-class swimming pools** to **eco-housing projects and working-class football teams**, the districts blend old Glasgow with emerging models of urban citizenship and sustainability.

They are not polished or picturesque, but they are **real, rooted, and rich with story**. They show us that regeneration isn't just about new buildings or sports arenas—it's about **dignity, memory, mutual care**, and the everyday work of communities building themselves from the ground up.

Their journey continues—not without struggle, but never without pride.

Chapter 4: The Southside - Identity, Diversity, and Change

4.1 Gorbals and Laurieston: Displacement and Design

4.1.1 Introduction: South of the River, At the Heart of the Story

When one crosses the **Clyde River** southward, they leave behind the iconic spires and mercantile façades of central Glasgow and enter an area that has long carried the weight of the city's most fraught urban experiments. The **Gorbals and Laurieston**, occupying a stretch just south of the river and west of the major artery that is the **A77 (Eglinton Street/Govan Road)**, have been cast and recast many times over the last two centuries: as working-class strongholds, as notorious slums, as architectural testbeds, and as blueprints for new visions of city life. Few districts in Glasgow have experienced such **cyclical upheaval, transformation, and reimagining**.

To understand Glasgow's modern identity—its social conscience, its housing legacy, its post-industrial realities—one must reckon with the story of the Gorbals and Laurieston. These neighbourhoods are not simply footnotes in the city's development: they are the **symbolic and physical epicentre** of its turbulent 20th-century urban narrative.

4.1.2 The Gorbals: From Overcrowded Slums to Urban Laboratory

19th-Century Foundations: Density, Diversity, and Desperation

In the 19th century, the Gorbals became one of Europe's most densely populated and ethnically mixed urban quarters. Fuelled by the **Industrial Revolution** and its proximity to the **Clyde's shipyards, mills, and ironworks**, it drew waves of working-class migrants:

- **Highland Scots** fleeing the clearances
- **Irish Catholics and Protestants** escaping famine and poverty
- **Jewish refugees** from Eastern Europe and Russia
- Later, **Italian**, **Lithuanian**, and **South Asian** communities

At its peak in the early 20th century, the Gorbals crammed over **90,000 people** into a single square mile. Families were housed in **unsanitary, multi-occupancy tenements**, lacking indoor plumbing, ventilation, or privacy. The resulting social conditions—poverty, disease, overcrowding, and crime—made the Gorbals infamous across the UK and a target for social reformers and city planners alike.

Cultural Life and Resilience

Despite its notoriety, the Gorbals was also a community of remarkable vibrancy. It birthed:

- Legendary **trade union leaders** and **Labour politicians**
- Rich **religious and cultural life**, especially through Catholic and Jewish institutions
- **Boxing gyms, music halls, corner shops**, and **oral storytelling traditions**

The residents shared a hard-won sense of identity rooted in **grit, humour, and neighbourliness**, and many would later lament the destruction not just of homes but of a unique **working-class ecosystem**.

4.1.3 Laurieston: Adjacent Yet Distinct

Immediately west of the Gorbals lies **Laurieston**, which was historically more industrial in character and slightly less populous. Laurieston served as a residential buffer between the Gorbals and more middle-class neighbourhoods like **Pollokshields**. It featured the same architectural characteristics—rows of red and blonde sandstone tenements—but was less dense and more varied in building stock.

In the mid-20th century, Laurieston too was swept into Glasgow's experimental **urban redevelopment schemes**, which tied its fate inexorably to that of its eastern neighbour.

4.1.4 Demolition and the Modernist Utopia That Failed

The Great Clearances (1950s–70s)

In post-WWII Britain, slum clearance became a national priority, and Glasgow's Gorbals stood as the ultimate test case. By the 1950s, planners declared the district unfit for human habitation. The city's response? A complete erasure of the Gorbals as it had existed.

- **Entire tenement blocks were razed**, sometimes overnight.
- Over **30,000 residents were displaced** to peripheral housing schemes—Easterhouse, Castlemilk, Drumchapel, and beyond.
- What remained was a void waiting for a new vision.

The Tower Blocks: Concrete Ambitions

In the 1960s, architects and city engineers built **Riverside and Hutchesontown**, vast experiments in **modernist housing**, driven by Brutalist aesthetics and promises of clean, vertical living. The most infamous of these was **Basil Spence's Hutchesontown C block**—a series of concrete towers designed to accommodate hundreds of families.

These were meant to elevate working-class life—both metaphorically and literally—but within two decades, most of them were seen as catastrophic failures:

- Poor construction and damp
- Social isolation and crime
- Degraded infrastructure and underinvestment

By the 1990s, most of the tower blocks had been demolished. What was meant to be a utopia became a symbol of **broken modernism and top-down planning hubris**.

4.1.5 New Gorbals: Design, Dignity, and Slow Transformation

The **New Gorbals** regeneration project, launched in the late 1990s, sought to do what 1960s planners had failed to: create an **urban neighbourhood that restored community fabric**, honoured design principles, and avoided both high-rise isolation and suburban sprawl.

Urban Design and Mixed Use

Key principles of the New Gorbals model included:

- **Low-rise, high-density architecture** echoing traditional tenement form
- **Integrated green spaces** and walkable streetscapes
- **Mixed tenure housing**, including social, shared ownership, and market-rate homes
- **Architectural variety**, with input from celebrated firms such as Elder & Cannon, Page\Park, and JM Architects

New buildings were given careful **aesthetic detailing** to avoid the institutional feel of earlier schemes. The area now includes:

- The award-winning **Civic Centre**, which houses libraries, health services, and council offices
- **St Francis Community Centre**, based in a restored 19th-century church
- **Landscaped courtyards** and public art that reference Gorbals' layered past

Community-Led Renewal

The regeneration also emphasised **participatory planning**:

- Tenants' associations and local organisations had real input into the design and allocation process.
- Former Gorbals residents were offered the chance to return—though many had settled elsewhere.
- Emphasis was placed on **community safety, youth programs, and social care** alongside bricks and mortar.

While still a work in progress, New Gorbals is now hailed internationally as a model of **urban renewal done with, not to, communities**.

4.1.6 Cultural Memory: What Was Lost and What Remains

The Gorbals lives on not just in street names but in **books, photography, oral histories, and myth**. It has been:

- Captured in the haunting images of **Oscar Marzaroli**, whose black-and-white photos from the 1960s remain iconic
- Immortalised in the plays of **Peter Mullan**, the poetry of **Liz Lochhead**, and documentaries like *Gorbals Children*
- Remembered in murals, such as the **Gorbals Vampire**—a real 1950s urban legend where children hunted a fictional creature in the Southern Necropolis

There's a fierce pride among those who lived through the old Gorbals, a sentiment best expressed in the refrain: **"We had nothing, but we had everything."**

4.1.7 Laurieston Today: Edges of Change

Laurieston has followed a slightly different regeneration path, but is now undergoing its own revitalisation as part of the **Laurieston Living project**, one of Glasgow's biggest current urban housing efforts.

- Phase by phase, new homes are being built, blending tenement aesthetics with modern insulation, sustainability, and communal space.

- **Crown Street** and its vicinity now include **public plazas, supermarkets, healthcare centres**, and **excellent transport links**, making it an increasingly desirable location.
- Art installations, like **colourful underpass murals** and **community mosaics**, soften the edges of ongoing construction and disruption.

Laurieston still grapples with the legacy of erasure—but the **integration of housing, infrastructure, and cultural planning** is a sign of a more thoughtful and holistic approach than past decades offered.

4.1.8 Conclusion: Gorbals and Laurieston as a Glasgow Parable

Together, the Gorbals and Laurieston tell the **story of Glasgow's housing policy in microcosm**—its deepest failures and most hopeful experiments. From the slums to the towers, from demolition to design-led rebirth, these neighbourhoods have lived through—and in many ways survived—every idea the city has had about what the urban working-class experience should look like.

Today, they are places of **ambition, tension, and human scale**—far from perfect, but undeniably alive. Their streets echo not just with the voices of the past, but with the ongoing conversation between residents, designers, and city officials about **what kind of place Glasgow wants to be**.

Their regeneration holds lessons not just for Scotland, but for cities across the world.

4.2 Tradeston to Kingston: Bridges, Brew Houses and Brutalism

4.2.1 Introduction: South of the River, Industrial Arteries and Urban Bones

Running along the **southern banks of the River Clyde,** from the western flank of the **Kingston Bridge** to the emerging creative zone around **Tradeston**, this stretch of the Southside may lack the postcard prettiness of the West End or the bustling multicultural vibrancy of Govanhill—but it is absolutely essential to understanding **Glasgow's industrial spine, transportation networks, and architectural evolution**. Here lie the remnants of **19th-century warehouses**, the shadows of **brutalist megastructures**, and the skeletons of old **brew houses and dock facilities** that once sustained Glasgow's economic dominance.

This riverside corridor is also a place of paradoxes: a land of **bridges and bypasses**, of **desolate post-industrial voids** now reawakened by ambitious regeneration schemes; a place where **historic granaries and old whisky bonds** sit beside modern apartments and digital hubs. From **brewery dynasties** to **post-war road engineering feats**, from **docks and dry goods** to **developers and digital creatives**, Tradeston and Kingston offer a layered, messy, and still-evolving portrait of Glasgow in motion.

4.2.2 Tradeston: Grains, Girders, and Glasgow's Granaries

The Victorian Industrial Core

By the mid-19th century, **Tradeston** had become a humming grid of warehouses, granaries, cooperages, ropeworks, and engineering yards. It owed its development to:

- Proximity to the Clyde, allowing direct access for **shipping grain, beer, timber, and machinery**
- An interlocking web of **railway sidings** and **canal infrastructure**, especially the **Paisley Canal Line**
- The rise of Glasgow as a global exporter of **coal, textiles, spirits**, and **heavy engineering components**

Companies like **J. & J. White Chemicals, Templetons**, and a number of **grain brokers and bonded warehouses** established a stronghold here. Some of the architectural footprints from this period—such as red-brick warehouses with iron window casements and heavy timber floors—still stand today, now retrofitted into mixed-use spaces.

Brew Houses and Spirits of the Southside

The Tradeston and Kingston area also sat at the edge of Glasgow's **historic brewing and distilling industries**. While most associate Scottish whisky with the Highlands or Speyside, the city once had dozens of distilleries and malt houses:

- The **Glasgow Distillery Company**, which originally had premises nearby, was one of many shuttered by the mid-20th century.
- Breweries like **Tennents (Wellpark Brewery)** had distribution warehouses and cooperages in the area.

Though brewing itself has largely left this district, echoes remain in **street names (Cooper Street, Malt Lane)** and surviving stone signage on older buildings.

4.2.3 Kingston: A Neighbourhood Beneath a Bridge

The area of **Kingston**, immediately west of Tradeston, was once a compact working-class neighbourhood with tenements and small-scale industry. Its identity was all but erased by **modern infrastructure projects**, particularly the **M8 motorway and Kingston Bridge**, which tore through communities in the 1960s and '70s.

The Kingston Bridge: Engineering Triumph, Urban Trauma

Opened in **1970**, the **Kingston Bridge** is one of Europe's busiest road bridges, carrying over **150,000 vehicles daily**. Spanning the Clyde and linking central Glasgow with the M8 corridor westwards toward Paisley and the airport, it was seen as the crown jewel of **post-war modernisation**.

But this engineering marvel came at a steep cost:

- **Entire communities in Kingston, Anderston, and parts of Tradeston were demolished** to make way for the motorway and access ramps.
- The surrounding space beneath and around the bridge became an **urban no-man's land**, dominated by **flyovers, parking lots, and neglected residual zones**.
- Homes were lost, pedestrian routes were severed, and community fabric disintegrated.

Today, the bridge looms not only as a feat of brutalist engineering, but also as a symbol of how **urban planning can erase rather than enhance place**.

4.2.4 Architecture of Industry and Brutalism

Tradeston and Kingston are home to a unique cross-section of Glasgow's architectural history, from **late Victorian warehouses** to **post-war concrete megastructures**.

Victorian Industrial Heritage

- Surviving examples of **grain warehouses**, many now converted into loft-style apartments or co-working spaces.
- The striking **Harvie & Hudson warehouse**, with its cast-iron columns and warehouse pulley mechanisms, now a protected building.
- A number of **B-listed facades**, particularly on Clyde Place and Commerce Street.

Brutalist Experiments and Civic Infrastructure

The post-war era brought **brutalist architecture**, often tied to state infrastructure:

- **Police offices, motorway flyovers**, and **transport nodes** that now dominate much of the skyline.
- **Bridge parapets, stairwells, underpasses**, and **multi-storey car parks**, defined by their **raw concrete massing**, geometric efficiency, and a now-unfashionable sense of monumentality.

While many of these structures are unloved today, they represent an important period of Glasgow's planning history and are increasingly subjects of **photographic and academic interest**.

4.2.5 Connectivity: Glasgow's Bridges and Mobility Crossroads

Few places in Glasgow illustrate the city's **transportation evolution** as clearly as this corridor.

Historic Bridges of the Clyde

Several bridges connect the south to the city centre:

- **George V Bridge (1928)** – an elegant arch bridge used by vehicles and buses.
- **Glasgow Suspension Bridge (1855)** – a graceful pedestrian bridge linking Carlton Place to the Saltmarket.
- **Squiggly Bridge (Tradeston Bridge, 2009)** – a contemporary pedestrian and cycle bridge named for its flowing curves; a symbol of the area's regeneration.

Each bridge tells a story of **technological ambition**, **changing modes of transport**, and **urban symbolism**—offering not just crossings, but perspectives on the evolving cityscape.

4.2.6 Urban Renewal: From Forgotten Edge to Digital Quarter

In the early 21st century, Glasgow began investing heavily in the regeneration of this forgotten corridor, with a vision to turn it into a **creative and technological hub**.

Tradeston's Transformation

- The **Clyde Place corridor** has seen warehouses repurposed into **design studios, art spaces, and start-up incubators**.
- The city introduced **street-level improvements**, such as lighting, walkways, and cycle paths, especially along the **Clyde Walkway**.
- In 2020, **Barclays Bank opened a massive new fintech campus**—the **Barclays Glasgow Campus**—bringing thousands of high-skilled jobs and international prestige to the Tradeston area.
- Supporting infrastructure includes **cafés, gyms, riverside promenades**, and improved transport links like the adjacent **Bridge Street Subway station**.

Public Art and Place-Making

Tradeston's rebranding also incorporates **public art, sculpture, and event space**, turning anonymous underpasses into more human-scale corridors.

- Murals on concrete pylons explore **Glasgow's industrial past** and **social diversity**.
- Pop-up events, temporary pavilions, and **outdoor performance spaces** have begun to animate previously dead zones.

4.2.7 Challenges and Critiques: Gentrification, Incompletion, and Disconnection

While Tradeston and Kingston are experiencing renewal, critics note persistent issues:

- **Physical barriers** like the M8 still sever these areas from both the city centre and Southside neighbourhoods.
- Gentrification threatens to displace long-standing small businesses and industrial users in favour of **corporate tenants and high-end flats**.
- The **urban fabric remains incomplete**: large swathes of land are still derelict or await development, and much of the architectural character has been lost.
- There's limited housing, meaning regeneration is commercial-heavy and lacks a truly lived-in feel.

Nonetheless, these areas are now once again **visible, talked about, and increasingly walked through**, a far cry from their status in the 1980s and '90s as **abandoned hinterlands**.

4.2.8 Conclusion: Concrete Past, Creative Future

From the rumble of cartwheels carrying barley to breweries, to the thunder of articulated lorries under the Kingston Bridge, from river ferries to digital start-ups—this corridor has witnessed Glasgow's most profound **shifts in industry, transport, architecture, and land use**.

Today, Tradeston and Kingston exist in a **transitional moment**: not quite fully reborn, but no longer ignored. They represent Glasgow's constant reinvention—a city always building, demolishing, and dreaming again. As bridges old and new span the Clyde, so too do these areas serve as symbolic crossings between **past and future, failure and possibility, grit and grace**.

4.3 Pollokshields and Govanhill: Glasgow's Global Neighborhoods

4.3.1 Introduction: Arrival, Adaptation, and Identity in the Southside

Pollokshields and Govanhill stand as two of Glasgow's most dynamic and culturally layered neighborhoods—distinct in character yet deeply intertwined in their **shared histories of immigration, urban diversity, working-class resilience, and social activism**. Both areas, located in the **Southern Inner Ring** of the city, have evolved into emblematic spaces of **Glasgow's global identity**, where voices from South Asia, Eastern Europe, the Middle East, Africa, and beyond mingle with the legacy of Victorian town planning and Scottish industrial history.

Together, they showcase the contradictions and possibilities of a modern, multicultural city: zones of deep **social cohesion and cultural richness**, yet also places marked by **chronic overcrowding, housing inequality, and complex demographic pressures**. They are as likely to host **mosques and gurdwaras** as old steepled churches, and their streets pulse with the aromas of **Pakistani bakeries, Polish grocers, Syrian cafés**, and long-standing Glaswegian chip shops.

Pollokshields—once one of Glasgow's wealthiest garden suburbs—offers a view of immigrant upward mobility, **Islamic architectural revivalism**, and civic pride. Govanhill, by contrast, stands at the coalface of **urban density, economic precarity**, and grassroots solidarity. Understanding these two neighborhoods is essential to understanding **Glasgow in the 21st century**.

4.3.2 Pollokshields: Garden Suburb, Spiritual Capital, and Cultural Mosaic

Origins as a Victorian Garden Suburb

Pollokshields was originally developed in the **mid-19th century** by the Stirling-Maxwell family as Glasgow's first **planned garden suburb**, intended as a residential haven for the city's wealthy merchant class. Its original layout, designed by architect **Alexander "Greek" Thomson**, emphasized:

- Broad, leafy avenues lined with **Victorian and Edwardian villas**, many featuring Greek Revival, Gothic, and Baronial architectural styles.
- Parks and green spaces such as **Maxwell Park**, intended to provide healthy living conditions away from the smoke-choked city centre.
- High architectural integrity, with numerous homes now **Category A or B listed** and preserved under the **Pollokshields Conservation Area**.

This architectural legacy remains a source of pride, offering a counterpoint to the urban density elsewhere in the Southside.

South Asian Settlement and the Emergence of 'Mini Lahore'

From the **1960s onward**, Pollokshields became a principal destination for **South Asian immigrants**, particularly from **Pakistan and India**, many of whom arrived under the **Commonwealth immigration schemes** or as professionals in sectors like medicine, transport, and engineering. Over time, the neighborhood earned its affectionate nickname: **"Mini Lahore"**.

Key developments include:

- The establishment of **mosques**, including the **Glasgow Central Mosque (1984)**—Scotland's largest and most prominent, located just outside Pollokshields—and the more local **Masjid Khazra**, **Jamia Islamia**, and **Masjid Noor**.
- The formation of an **economically vibrant Pakistani and Bangladeshi business community**, with restaurants, sari shops, Islamic bookstores, and halal butchers lining Allison Street and Albert Drive.
- An increased emphasis on **religious education, community centres, and Islamic schools**, including the **Iqra Learning Centre** and **Al Meezan Centre**, which promote Islamic scholarship, women's outreach, and youth engagement.

The area is known for its **intergenerational family homes**, often converted or extended, supporting **strong kinship networks** that blur the lines between private and public space.

Civic Activism and Interfaith Dialogue

Pollokshields is also home to a **strong civic consciousness**. Community organisations have been at the forefront of:

- **Anti-racism and anti-deportation campaigns**, such as the widely publicised **Kenmure Street protest in 2021**, where hundreds of local residents prevented the Home Office from detaining two Sikh men.
- **Interfaith efforts**, including open-mosque days, Christian-Muslim dialogues, and charity drives co-organised by gurdwaras, mosques, and churches.
- Initiatives around **urban gardening, environmental sustainability**, and housing preservation, including the **Pollokshields Trust** and **Pollokshields Heritage** groups.

This fusion of cultural preservation and progressive politics gives the area a **distinctly self-aware and globally conscious identity**.

4.3.3 Govanhill: Migration, Multitudes, and the Struggles of Density

19th-Century Roots and Industrial Growth

Originally a village on the outskirts of Glasgow, Govanhill rapidly urbanised during the **Industrial Revolution**, when its location near **coal mines, textile factories, and tramway yards** made it an ideal site for working-class housing. The area became a hub for:

- **Red sandstone tenements**, packed tightly into grids with shared backcourts and washhouses.
- Early 20th-century tram lines and the **Coplawhill tram depot**, which provided mass transit across the city.
- A diverse population of **Irish immigrants, Jewish families**, and internal Scottish migrants drawn by work in heavy industry.

Its tenements, while architecturally impressive, were often **overcrowded and poorly maintained**, laying the foundation for the urban struggles that continue today.

Post-2000 Waves of Migration and Ethnic Complexity

In the 21st century, Govanhill has emerged as **Scotland's most ethnically diverse neighbourhood**, with an estimated **88 different languages spoken** and over **50 nationalities represented**. Major demographic shifts include:

- **Roma communities from Slovakia, Romania, and the Czech Republic**, who began settling in large numbers in the early 2000s, often in substandard private housing.
- Continued growth of **South Asian populations**, particularly Muslim and Sikh communities, overlapping with those in nearby Pollokshields.
- Arrival of **asylum seekers and refugees** from Syria, Afghanistan, Sudan, and Eritrea, supported by organisations like the **Scottish Refugee Council**.
- Longstanding **Scottish and Irish Catholic residents**, many of whom retain deep intergenerational ties to the neighborhood.

This rich demographic tapestry contributes to Govanhill's vibrant street life, with **markets, cafés, and informal economies** operating in visible and invisible ways throughout the neighborhood.

Social Struggles and Community Solidarity

Govanhill has faced well-documented challenges, including:

- **Overcrowded and unsafe housing**, exacerbated by rogue landlords and limited council capacity.
- **Tensions over sanitation, anti-social behaviour, and public space**, often sensationalised in media coverage.
- **Public health issues**, including infestations, poor drainage, and inconsistent rubbish collection.

In response, the neighborhood has developed **remarkably strong community infrastructure**, including:

- The **Govanhill Baths Community Trust**, which saved and now runs the once-derelict Victorian baths as a centre for arts, activism, and wellness.
- **Govanhill Community Development Trust**, providing support for housing, tenancy rights, and cultural integration.
- **Language cafés, cultural festivals**, and **anti-racist campaigning groups** promoting unity across divides.

Govanhill's challenges have fostered a **resilient and activist spirit**, making it a place where grassroots action is the norm, not the exception.

4.3.4 Shared Spaces: Culture, Cuisine, and Everyday Cosmopolitanism

Walking through Govanhill and Pollokshields, one is immersed in a **daily cosmopolitanism** rarely found elsewhere in the UK. Features of this living, breathing multiculturalism include:

- **Spice shops, African hair salons, Polish delis**, and Romanian mobile phone stores all operating side-by-side.
- Community kitchens that offer **free meals for migrants and the unhoused**, supported by Sikh langar initiatives and Muslim charitable kitchens.
- An eclectic blend of **religious architecture**, including mosques, gurdwaras, Hindu mandirs, and former churches now serving diverse congregations.

Annual events like the **Southside Fringe Festival, Govanhill International Festival**, and **Eid in the Park** celebrations help knit together these populations in celebration and solidarity.

4.3.5 Contrasts, Tensions, and the Politics of Place

Though close in geography, Pollokshields and Govanhill reveal **sharply contrasting dynamics**:

- **Pollokshields** often represents **settled diaspora prosperity**, marked by homeownership, religious infrastructure, and political capital.
- **Govanhill**, by contrast, reflects **constant flux, economic vulnerability, and high rental churn**.

This contrast reveals deep questions about:

- **Urban inclusion**—who gets to belong and who gets blamed?
- **Gentrification**—as artists and developers eye parts of Govanhill, will rents rise and displace the very communities that gave it character?
- **State presence**—how should councils and governments intervene in such a complex urban matrix?

4.3.6 Conclusion: A Tale of Two Neighborhoods, One Global City

Pollokshields and Govanhill are **microcosms of 21st-century Glasgow**: global in population, local in spirit, and complex in lived experience. They are not easy to summarise, nor are they without contradiction. But in their mosques and bathhouses, takeaways and temples, protests and community halls, one finds the soul of a city that **continues to welcome, struggle, adapt, and endure**.

These neighborhoods do not merely house Glasgow's immigrants—they **shape the city's identity, politics, and future**. They are not peripheries but frontlines, where culture is not curated but lived. And in their lived, imperfect, multicoloured sprawl, they remind us that **the story of Glasgow is far from finished**.

4.4 Queen's Park, Strathbungo and Shawlands: Southside Soul and Suburbia

4.4.1 Introduction: The Southside's Cultural Arc

Nestled in the heart of Glasgow's Southside, the districts of **Queen's Park**, **Strathbungo**, and **Shawlands** form a richly layered cultural corridor that blends **Victorian suburbia, green expanses, creative vibrancy, and commercial reinvention**. This area represents the **soulful pulse of middle-class Glasgow**, combining genteel urban planning and architectural charm with modern-day reinvention through cafes, galleries, and grassroots community events.

While each neighborhood retains its distinct character—Queen's Park with its civic grandeur and public parkland, Strathbungo with its tight-knit conservation terraces and bohemian energy, and Shawlands with its dynamic high street and growing cosmopolitanism—the area as a whole forms a **nexus of lifestyle, heritage, and progressive culture** in the city. Over the past two decades, this triangle has become a sought-after postcode for **young professionals, artists, academics, and diverse immigrant communities**, drawn to its connectivity, authenticity, and greenery.

As gentrification brushes up against a deep historical texture, the Southside's arc from **Victorian garden suburb to hip urban quarter** is nowhere more evident than here.

4.4.2 Queen's Park: Public Space, Political Memory, and Everyday Life

The Park and Its Origins

Queen's Park, laid out in the 1850s by the celebrated landscape designer **Sir Joseph Paxton**, is one of Glasgow's grandest civic parks—an elevated, 148-acre green space designed for both **recreation and reflection**. Named after **Mary, Queen of Scots**, the park was designed to offer open-air leisure to the growing urban middle classes of South Glasgow and has long functioned as a democratic space for **public gathering, performance, and protest**.

Key features include:

- **The Glasshouse**, a 19th-century iron-and-glass structure (now undergoing restoration), once used for tropical botany and community events.
- The **flagpole viewpoint**, offering panoramic views over the city and as far as Ben Lomond on a clear day.
- Historic remnants of the **Battle of Langside (1568)**, the last confrontation between Mary, Queen of Scots and forces loyal to her son James VI, with markers commemorating this pivotal moment in Scottish history.
- Modern-day uses such as **farmer's markets**, art festivals, impromptu gigs, and youth skateboarding.

The park also serves as a psychological and geographic anchor for surrounding neighborhoods—**a green lung** around which everyday life orbits.

The Civic and Cultural Role

Queen's Park has long been a stage for political life and cultural activism. In the 20th century, it hosted:

- **Labour and socialist rallies**, especially during the Red Clydeside era.
- Marches and memorials during the **Poll Tax protests**, anti-war vigils, and environmental campaigns.

- Open-air performances and the beloved **Queen's Park Arena**, now revitalised with new programming including film screenings, LGBTQ+ events, and children's theatre.

The park's very landscape—equal parts rolling lawn and rugged woodland—mirrors the layered nature of Southside society: communal, aspirational, and historically self-aware.

4.4.3 Strathbungo: Conservation, Creativity, and Community

Victorian Urbanism and the Birth of a 'Model Suburb'

Strathbungo—originally a feuing estate on the lands of Shields—evolved in the mid-to-late 19th century as a highly planned, architecturally unified suburb, largely driven by the hand of **Alexander "Greek" Thomson** and his contemporaries. The area showcases:

- Uniform **terraced townhouses in honeyed blonde and red sandstone**, many now listed for preservation.
- Narrow lanes, communal gardens, and discreet crescents that reflect a **residential intimacy**, rare in the city's larger grid.

- A Conservation Area designation protecting Strathbungo's elegant spatial rhythm and coherent scale.

From its inception, Strathbungo has straddled **working-class roots and bourgeois elegance**, housing artisans, shopkeepers, and professionals in proximity—an ethos that continues today.

The Rise of a Creative Micro-Hub

In the 21st century, Strathbungo has carved out a reputation as a **creative and community-minded enclave**, home to:

- A disproportionately high number of **musicians, artists, designers, and writers**, many of whom are active in local cultural programming.
- Events like **Bungo in the Back Lanes**, a summer street festival where residents open their gardens to stalls, performances, and food sharing—epitomising grassroots urbanism.
- The **Strathbungo Society**, a leading community organisation promoting conservation, placemaking, and collective memory through events, oral history, and local campaigning.
- The **Shawlands & Strathbungo Community Council**, which plays a vocal role in development decisions, transport access, and sustainability plans.

This is a neighborhood where **front steps double as concert stages**, where public art appears on hoardings, and where the line between private and public life is creatively blurred.

4.4.4 Shawlands: Suburban Heart, Commercial Spine

From Tram Terminus to Urban Village

Shawlands began its ascent in the **early 20th century**, flourishing as a **tram-linked suburb** offering middle-class families modern flats, nearby parks, and direct access to the city centre. Shawlands Cross, with its iconic clock tower, became a central node around which shops, services, cinemas, and banks clustered.

Today, Shawlands functions as the **commercial and transport hub** of the Southside, with key arteries such as **Kilmarnock Road, Pollokshaws Road, and Minard Road** forming a buzzing triangle of activity. Notable features include:

- The **Granary**, **The Glad Café**, and **Lagom Kitchen**—venues that mix food, performance, and social gathering.

- A rich tapestry of **independent boutiques, vegan eateries, craft beer pubs**, and post offices, all coexisting.
- Access to **Pollok Park, Queen's Park, and Langside Hall**, making Shawlands feel both urban and green.

The area's continued development has led some to dub it the **"Southside West End"**, though locals often resist this framing in favour of its **own, less self-conscious charm**.

Gentrification, Inclusion, and Local Activism

Shawlands has experienced a **clear uptick in property values, renovations, and demographic change**, but this has sparked:

- Concerns about the **displacement of working-class residents**, particularly around former social housing clusters.
- Strong campaigns to **retain public services and affordable shops**, with initiatives such as Shawlands Business Improvement District (BID) and **community buyouts** of threatened spaces.
- A growing **multi-ethnic presence**, with South Asian, Eastern European, and African communities adding to the area's street life and food culture.

There is an ongoing tension between **curated lifestyle aesthetics** and organic diversity—a dynamic that animates local debates over urban design, retail chains, and nightlife.

4.4.5 Southside Soul: Arts, Identity, and the Everyday

Beyond the architectural and commercial, this trio of neighborhoods embodies an intangible spirit—a sense of **Southside soul** that plays out in:

- **Creative placemaking**, seen in window displays, poetry corners, and spontaneous gigs.
- **Intergenerational continuity**, with long-standing families sharing space with newcomers, all finding common ground in community schools, cafés, and bus stops.
- A **progressive political identity**, with many residents voting for Green and SNP candidates, supporting independence, refugee rights, and climate action.

The Southside's cultural life is deeply participatory. Whether through **art trails**, **parent-run schools initiatives**, or **queer community meetups**, this is an area that **lives out its values in everyday ways**—often quietly, always persistently.

4.4.6 Conclusion: A Southside That Looks Forward

Queen's Park, Strathbungo, and Shawlands represent the **most compelling case study of South Glasgow's evolution** from Victorian suburbia to a living, breathing cultural engine of the modern city. These neighborhoods showcase:

- The adaptive reuse of green space and historic homes.
- The integration of migration, art, and community activism into everyday life.
- A balancing act between heritage preservation and dynamic change.

They are not perfect places—there are housing pressures, infrastructural gaps, and affordability challenges—but they are **deeply lived-in and fiercely loved**. In their mixture of **diversity, design, and defiance**, they offer not just shelter but meaning—a way of life that **defies urban anonymity** and insists on civic connection.

If the Southside has a soul, it is found here—in the terrace back gardens, the protest on the green, the latte shared between languages, and the mural on the butcher's wall.

Chapter 5: Glasgow Lives – Stories, Struggles, and Strength

5.1 Epilogue – The Future of Glasgow: A City Still in the Making

5.1.1 Introduction: A City at a Crossroads

Glasgow is a city forever in motion—a place whose identity is built not on stasis or perfection, but on reinvention. From its medieval ecclesiastical core to its mighty shipyards, from Victorian grandeur to post-industrial decline and contemporary rebirth, Glasgow has rarely remained still. As we reach this concluding chapter, we must ask: what lies ahead for a city so shaped by turbulence, tenacity, and transformation?

The future of Glasgow is **not a straight line**, nor is it a simple narrative of recovery or progress. It is **messy, contested, hopeful**, and full of contradictions. It is a story being shaped in the tenements of Govanhill, the innovation hubs of Finnieston, the classrooms of Maryhill, and the community gardens of Castlemilk. It is carried in the struggles for affordable housing, the campaigns for climate justice, the poetry of youth, and the resolve of old unions repurposed for new fights.

Glasgow's motto still reads "Let Glasgow Flourish," but the unspoken question remains—**on whose terms?** For whom? And in what image?

5.1.2 The End of Industry, The Rise of Innovation?

One of the most defining forces shaping Glasgow's trajectory is the **long shadow of deindustrialisation**. The collapse of shipbuilding, manufacturing, mining, and heavy engineering in the late 20th century fractured not only the economy but the **social contracts and cultural identities** that came with it. Whole communities were uprooted; employment became precarious, and multigenerational trades disappeared almost overnight.

In response, Glasgow turned to **the 'new economy': tourism, culture, education, and tech**. The city rebranded itself as a **centre for events and innovation**—hosting the 1990 European City of Culture, the 2014 Commonwealth Games, and COP26 in 2021. Post-industrial landscapes like the Clyde waterfront, Merchant City, and East End were reimagined through the language of **urban regeneration**, enterprise zones, and creative districts.

Yet this shift brought **winners and losers**. While parts of Glasgow flourished with new investment, others remained caught in cycles of deprivation. The digital revolution offers possibilities, but it also exacerbates inequalities between those with access and skills, and those without. Glasgow's future as a knowledge economy must be weighed against the lived realities of **postcode poverty**, exclusion, and uneven spatial development.

Will Glasgow continue to build a city based on glossy precincts and tech corridors, or will it prioritise **inclusive growth that uplifts forgotten neighbourhoods**?

5.1.3 Housing, Land, and the Right to the City

At the heart of Glasgow's future lies a fundamental struggle: **who has the right to the city?** As demand grows and housing becomes increasingly financialised, questions of ownership, affordability, and displacement are coming to the fore.

Glasgow has both **Europe's largest council housing stock** and some of its most severe housing stress. Despite award-winning regeneration schemes like the **Gorbals and Laurieston redesign**, areas such as Possilpark, Easterhouse, and Drumchapel continue to struggle with **substandard housing, homelessness, and dereliction**.

Meanwhile, urban land—long held by private entities, often absentee—is increasingly a **battleground between developers and communities**. Across the city, residents are demanding a say in what happens to their parks, high streets, and abandoned plots. Initiatives such as:

- The **Govanhill Community Development Trust**
- The **People's Plan for Candleriggs**
- The **GalGael Trust's reclaiming of skills and land in Govan**

...signal a **growing movement for democratic control** of urban space.

The future of Glasgow depends not only on what is built, but **how it is built—and who it is built for**. Can a city with a history of exploitative urban clearance and speculative development learn from its past to craft a more participatory, community-led model of growth?

5.1.4 Climate Change and the City's Green Future

The climate emergency will define Glasgow's path forward in ways both visible and hidden. From **flood-prone riverbanks to carbon-heavy transport systems**, the city must adapt at every level. During COP26, the world's eyes turned to Glasgow—not only as host, but as a test case of how post-industrial cities can become climate-resilient and just.

Key challenges and opportunities include:

- Retrofitting **Victorian and 20th-century housing stock** to be energy efficient
- Expanding and protecting **green spaces and biodiversity corridors**
- Replacing car-centric planning with **active transport infrastructure**—cycleways, pedestrian-friendly streets, and better public transport
- Investing in **clean energy jobs** and community renewable schemes

The city's future will require **bold decisions** and **collective action**, avoiding the greenwashing of elite projects in favour of **grassroots climate justice**—where the most vulnerable communities are not burdened, but empowered.

Glasgow must ask: will environmental policy be top-down and technocratic—or locally rooted and socially just?

5.1.5 Migration, Identity, and the City That Welcomes

Few cities in Britain have as rich and complex a migration story as Glasgow. From the **Highland Clearances, Irish and Italian migration**, to post-war arrivals from **Pakistan, the Caribbean, and Eastern Europe**, the city has been continually reshaped by movement and mixing. Today, Govanhill is said to be home to over **60 languages**, and communities from **Syria, Ukraine, and Sudan** are weaving new threads into the city's tapestry.

Glasgow has declared itself a **City of Sanctuary**, proud to welcome asylum seekers and refugees. The work of organisations such as:

- **Positive Action in Housing**
- **Refuweegee**
- **Unity Centre**

...has built an infrastructure of solidarity, even as the UK's hostile environment policies make life difficult for newcomers.

The future of Glasgow is unmistakably **multicultural**, but the task remains to ensure **representation, equity, and cultural flourishing**—not merely tolerance. How will the next generation of Glaswegians see themselves—as hyphenated identities, as Scots with global roots, or as new voices shaping the mainstream?

5.1.6 Young People and the City to Come

Glasgow's future is in the hands of its **young people**—many of whom are deeply aware of inequality, climate anxiety, mental health challenges, and political disillusionment. Yet they are also the architects of a more radical, more just, and more hopeful vision of the city.

Across schools, youth centres, collectives, and protests, young Glaswegians are demanding:

- **Action on racism, sexism, and LGBTQ+ rights**
- **Free and equitable education**
- **Mental health resources without stigma**
- **Decent housing and job prospects**
- **Decolonisation of public space and curriculum**

Their activism—from climate strikes to street murals, from spoken word to citizen journalism—is shaping public discourse in new ways. The city's institutions must listen—not simply co-opt these voices into token roles, but **make space for youth leadership** in policy, planning, and cultural life.

Will Glasgow empower its young people not just to speak—but to decide?

5.1.7 Conclusion: A City Still Becoming

Glasgow is not finished. It never has been.

It is a city of fragments and futures, of hard-won pride and unresolved wounds. It is a city whose heart beats not in monuments or slogans, but in the **daily struggle of its people to make a life, to make beauty, to make change**. It is as much about the community centre as the concert hall, the bus stop as the boardroom, the spoken word as the architectural blueprint.

To imagine Glasgow's future is not to project a single vision—but to embrace its **plurality, its dynamism, and its contradictions**. It is to understand that this city thrives not in spite of its messiness, but because of it. The old industrial smoke may have lifted, but the fire of **working-class resilience, creative reinvention, and collective care** still burns.

The epilogue, in truth, is a **prologue**. The city remains unfinished. And that is exactly its power.

Let Glasgow Flourish—**on new terms, by new voices, for new generations**.

5.2 Oral Histories and Local Legends: Listening to the City's Soul

5.2.1 Introduction: Beyond the Official Record

The story of Glasgow is not only found in its architecture, archives, or official histories. It lives in the **spoken word**, the **remembered fragments**, and the **half-whispered myths** passed down across kitchen tables, street corners, pubs, and community centres. These are the stories rarely recorded in books—yet they echo most powerfully through the city's identity.

Oral histories and local legends offer a **people's version of Glasgow**—often messier, more emotional, more contradictory than institutional narratives, but also more intimate and revealing. These stories shed light on **hidden experiences**: of migration and hardship, humour and hope, violence and resilience. In them, we hear the city not as a fixed place but as a **living voice**—arguing, laughing, remembering, and dreaming.

In a place shaped by poverty, protest, migration, and industry, oral history is not a luxury. It is a survival tool, a record of dignity, and a resistance to forgetting.

5.2.2 Tenement Tales: Living Close, Living Loud

For generations of Glaswegians, life unfolded in the tight corridors and shared stairwells of **tenement housing**. These spaces bred a distinct form of urban intimacy: **stories shouted from balconies**, tales swapped over communal washing lines, and childhood adventures mapped across back greens and closes.

Older residents still recall:

- **Women who "kept an eye" on every child** in the building, not as busybodies, but as unpaid sentinels of communal safety.
- The **boiler rooms and coal bunkers** that doubled as childhood hideouts and storytelling dens.
- Nighttime tales of **"the wee man in the loft"** or **the ghost of the coal chute** that terrified youngsters into staying indoors.

These tenement tales reveal more than nostalgia—they illustrate how people made **community out of constraint,** and turned overcrowding into kinship.

5.2.3 Working-Class Memory and Political Fire

Glasgow's oral traditions carry a fierce political charge. It is a city where memories of **strikes, unions, marches, and mutual aid** live on in every neighbourhood.

In Govan, locals remember their grandparents' tales of the **Upper Clyde Shipbuilders' Work-In of 1971**, when workers occupied the yards to protest closures. These weren't just political moments—they were **acts of defiance wrapped in daily life**: sandwiches carried to shipbuilders, children marching beside parents, songs sung at the gates.

In Bridgeton, stories of the **Red Clydeside era** are passed down with pride—of "Big John Maclean," of the mass protests on Glasgow Green, of the time when the city stood **on the edge of revolution**. Local elders often recall:

"We didnae need tae read about socialism—we lived it."

These stories, told over generations, are part of **Glasgow's radical DNA**—a reminder that resistance didn't always look like headlines; often, it looked like **small acts of care, refusal, and courage**.

5.2.4 Women's Voices: From Domesticity to Defiance

Oral history in Glasgow also reclaims the voices of **working-class women**, too often marginalised in official narratives. Across the city, especially in communities like Pollok, Castlemilk, Maryhill, and the Gorbals, women have long been the **backbone of survival, organisers of resistance**, and keepers of community knowledge.

Common themes emerge:

- **Rationing and resilience** during and after the war—how women "made do" and built networks of trade, reuse, and mutual support.
- **Rent strikes**, especially the famous 1915 Glasgow Rent Strike, led by women like **Mary Barbour**, remembered not only for victory, but for the fierce neighbourhood organisation behind it.
- Everyday rituals: the importance of **"the message" (shopping), "a fly cup" (a tea and gossip)**, and **support groups born in laundrettes and bus queues**.

Many Glaswegian women speak of growing up with few resources, but with **rich cultural memory**—storytelling, songs, and sayings passed from mothers to daughters.

These oral histories **re-centre Glasgow's women as community leaders**, moral historians, and builders of urban solidarity.

5.2.5 Migrant Memories: Layers of Belonging

Glasgow's layers of migration have created a vibrant mosaic of oral culture. Each wave—Irish, Jewish, Italian, Pakistani, African-Caribbean, Roma, Eastern European, Syrian—has brought not just labour and food, but **stories**: of exile, hope, trauma, and home-making.

In Pollokshields, older residents remember the **first mosques**, the importance of halal butchers, and the mixed emotions of arrival: welcome from some neighbours, hostility from others. One often-heard story is of immigrant families attending ceilidhs and football matches as ways of blending in—**hybrid rituals that created a new Glaswegian identity**.

In Govanhill, Roma families pass down **tales of travel, persecution, and perseverance**, speaking multiple languages while planting roots on Glasgow soil. Many of these oral stories are not written down—but are enacted in family meals, music, and parenting styles.

The oral culture of migrants reveals how Glasgow is not a "melting pot" that flattens difference, but a **city of multiple, coexisting narratives**—often overlapping in unexpected and beautiful ways.

5.2.6 Ghost Stories, Myths, and Urban Legends

Beyond factual memory, Glasgow is filled with a rich tradition of **urban legends**—some humorous, some chilling, some plainly absurd, but all revealing the fears, humour, and personality of the city.

Classic local legends include:

- The **Grey Lady of the Necropolis**, a veiled ghost said to roam the tombstones, appearing to those mourning the recently deceased.
- The **Gorbals Vampire Panic of 1954**, when dozens of children searched Southern Necropolis for a seven-foot vampire believed to have iron teeth. (In

truth, it was sparked by horror comics—but it reflects how urban myths shape youth culture and media fear.)

- **"The White Lady of Bellgrove"**, who appears at the site of a tragic fire, said to warn against greed or wrongdoing.
- Tales of secret tunnels beneath Glasgow Cathedral and the University cloisters, often told with nods to smugglers, ghosts, or Jacobite hideaways.

These stories, however embellished, are windows into the **collective imagination**—ways of dealing with danger, mystery, and power. They are part of the city's folklore, passed down in whispers or dramatized by local actors and schools.

5.2.7 The Pub as Archive: Memory on Tap

In Glasgow, the **public house** has long served as more than a place to drink—it is an **unofficial archive**, a stage for storytelling, myth-making, and memory-sharing.

In places like **The Laurieston, The Scotia Bar**, and **The Clutha**, patrons gather not just for pints but to recount tales of:

- The man who once drank with Billy Connolly "before he was famous"
- The time Alex Ferguson was nearly refused service at a pub in Govan
- Legendary gigs, bar fights, marriages, and reconciliations born under neon lights

These tales often blur the line between **truth and exaggeration**, but they are treated as sacred nonetheless. They represent a **social currency**, and the pub itself becomes a **repository of working-class oral tradition**.

5.2.8 Oral Histories in Action: Projects and Preservation

Recognising the value of oral history, several groups have worked to **collect, preserve, and celebrate** these stories:

- **Glasgow Women's Library** runs intergenerational storytelling sessions and oral history workshops.
- **The Scottish Oral History Centre (University of Strathclyde)** documents working lives, migration, health, and housing.
- **Remembering the Gorbals, Voices from Easterhouse**, and **Govan Reminiscence Group** are just a few examples of community-driven archives that protect memory from erasure.
- **Refuweegee**, a contemporary storytelling project, invites new Glaswegians to share their first impressions and layered identities.

These initiatives ensure that **oral histories are not just nostalgia**, but active parts of civic life—tools for education, empathy, and change.

5.2.9 Conclusion: The Soul of Glasgow, Spoken and Shared

Glasgow's essence lies not just in what it has built, but in **what its people remember**—and how they tell it. From whispered ghost stories to shouted protest chants, from ceilidhs to corner shop conversations, the city is held together by **a million voices**, many of them never published or broadcast.

To listen to Glasgow's soul is to tune into its diversity, its humour, its rage, its care. It means valuing a retired nurse's account as much as an official historian's. It means recognising that a child's story of growing up in a tower block holds **as much urban wisdom** as any city plan.

In oral history, Glasgow comes alive—not as a museum, but as a moving, breathing, speaking city.

Let us listen, before the voices fade. Let us remember, before the stories are lost. Let Glasgow flourish—not just in buildings and budgets—but in **its voices, memories, and everyday legends**.

5.3 Migrations and Memories: Journeys That Shaped the City

5.3.1 Introduction: Glasgow as a City of Movement

To understand Glasgow is to understand **movement**—of people, cultures, and stories across borders and generations. Migration has never been an exception in Glasgow's history; it is the rule. The city's soul is not singular or static but shaped by **waves of arrivals**: some welcomed, some resisted, but all leaving a mark. The legacies of these journeys—some voluntary, many forced—are etched into the bricks of tenements, the rhythms of speech, the spices in the food, and the prayers said in churches, synagogues, mosques, gurdwaras, and temples across the city.

From the **Highland Clearances** to **postcolonial diasporas**, from **economic migrants** to **asylum seekers**, Glasgow has offered refuge, opportunity, and community, even as it has also dealt out hardship, xenophobia, and struggle. What emerges from these many movements is not a seamless multicultural utopia, but a rich, layered, often difficult tapestry of identity—held together by memory, pride, resilience, and adaptation.

This chapter examines the **migrations that built Glasgow**, not just economically, but emotionally and culturally. Through personal memory, neighbourhood transformation, and community organisation, we explore the journeys that continue to shape and redefine what it means to be a Glaswegian.

5.3.2 Irish Glasgow: A City Within a City

Perhaps no migration has defined Glasgow more enduringly than that of the **Irish**, especially during the **Great Famine** of the mid-19th century. By the 1850s, it was estimated that **one in four Glaswegians** was Irish-born. They settled primarily in the East End and Gorbals, often enduring horrific housing conditions, dangerous labour, and virulent anti-Catholic sentiment.

But their cultural imprint was—and remains—massive:

- The development of **Catholic institutions**: schools, churches, and charities that would support generations of new arrivals.
- The rise of **Celtic Football Club** in 1887 by Irish Marist Brother Walfrid to help feed the poor in the East End.
- **Labour organising and left-wing politics**, where Irish Glaswegians were active in union struggles and anti-fascist movements.

Despite integration, sectarianism lingered, sometimes violently. Yet Irish-Scots families often speak of a dual identity: **fiercely Glaswegian, proudly Irish**, with grandparents who spoke in County Donegal lilts and great-uncles who marched in the 1970s for miners' rights.

Today, that legacy continues through Irish music nights in pubs, Gaelic Masses in Dennistoun, and family names that bridge two histories.

5.3.3 Jewish Journeys: From Eastern Europe to the Gorbals

In the late 19th and early 20th centuries, **Jewish migrants from Eastern Europe**, fleeing pogroms and persecution in Tsarist Russia and Poland, arrived in Glasgow in significant numbers. Many settled in the **Gorbals**, transforming its streets into a hub of **kosher butchers, Yiddish newspapers, tailors' workshops**, and religious life.

The Jewish community:

- Brought skilled trades and educational ambition, contributing significantly to Glasgow's middle class by the mid-20th century.
- Built vibrant institutions like the **Garnethill Synagogue** and **Jewish Institute**, a cornerstone of cultural life.
- Created a legacy of civic leadership in law, medicine, and politics.

Though much of the original Gorbals Jewish community dispersed in later decades to suburbs like Giffnock and Newton Mearns, older residents recall vividly the warmth, humour, and deep religiosity of the neighbourhood. Oral histories often blend Yiddish expressions with Gorbals slang—a unique dialect born of diaspora and industrial proximity.

Today, Glasgow's Jewish community remains one of the largest in Scotland, with a firm grasp on **memory as a form of continuity**.

5.3.4 South Asian Migration: Partition and Postcolonial Glasgow

Following the **end of British rule in India and Pakistan in 1947**, and especially during the 1950s–70s, **South Asian migration** reshaped Glasgow's demographic and cultural landscape. Many early migrants came as **students, factory workers, and business owners**, often facing difficult housing conditions and outright racism.

Pollokshields and Govanhill became major hubs, where families from **Punjab, Gujarat, Bengal, and later Bangladesh** settled. Their impact was felt in:

- The rise of **corner shops**, textile wholesalers, and curry houses—hallmarks of postwar urban life in Glasgow.
- The creation of Glasgow's **first mosques**, Hindu temples, Sikh gurdwaras, and community centres.
- A generation of **British-born Asians** who carved space in education, politics, and culture, while still navigating exclusion.

Memories of early settlement tell of **multiple layers of negotiation**—between cultures, languages, religions, and identity. Many recall the difficulty of being told to "go back home," despite having no memory of anywhere else. And yet, a **resilient civic identity** emerged—where families celebrated Eid and Diwali while supporting Partick Thistle or marching against Thatcher's policies.

Today, the South Asian diaspora is woven deeply into Glasgow's fabric—from kebab shops to Bhangra nights, from city councillors to poets.

5.3.5 African-Caribbean and Black Scottish Identity

Though small in numbers, the **African and Caribbean presence in Glasgow** has a long and often overlooked history, stretching back to the **colonial period and maritime trade**. Sailors, students, and later migrants from the **Windrush generation** came to the Clyde, often finding work on ships, in hospitals, or in transport.

Glasgow's Black community:

- Faced **institutional racism and social isolation**, but built support through churches, clubs, and community activism.
- Gave rise to voices like **Sir Geoff Palmer**, the pioneering scientist and campaigner, and **Jackie Kay**, the poet whose life story interweaves race, adoption, and belonging in Glasgow.
- Created a Black Scottish identity that is both proud and politically engaged, especially in modern antiracist and refugee solidarity movements.

Today, Black Scottish youth in Glasgow are leading conversations about **colonial history, identity, and decolonisation**—redefining the city's sense of itself.

5.3.6 Eastern European Migration: Post-EU Glasgow

With the **2004 enlargement of the European Union**, Glasgow saw a significant influx of **Eastern European migrants**, especially **Poles, Slovakians, Lithuanians, and Romanians**. Many arrived to fill labour shortages in construction, care work, and hospitality.

Their presence is evident in:

- New shops and bakeries in Govanhill, Ibrox, and Partick, selling pierogi, kabanos, and rye bread.
- Cultural events and language schools keeping heritage alive while children become fluent Glaswegians.
- Tensions and solidarity within existing migrant groups, as economic pressures mount.

While some have returned to their countries post-Brexit, many have stayed and are raising a new generation of bilingual Glaswegians—children who speak Polish at home and Scots in the playground.

5.3.7 Asylum, Sanctuary, and Solidarity

In the 21st century, Glasgow has become one of the **UK's main dispersal cities** for asylum seekers and refugees. From **Iraq, Syria, Iran, Sudan, Eritrea, and Afghanistan**, thousands have come here seeking safety—and faced a difficult path marked by trauma, bureaucracy, and hostility.

Yet, Glasgow has also become a city of sanctuary:

- Organisations like **Positive Action in Housing**, **Refuweegee**, and **Scottish Refugee Council** offer vital support.
- Schoolchildren welcome classmates from across the world—often before adults in power do.
- Refugee-led projects in arts, food, and storytelling are flourishing, adding new voices to the city's evolving narrative.

Many refugee families speak of Glasgow as the **first place they felt welcome**—not always by systems, but by **neighbours**. A Syrian mother recalls, "The woman upstairs brought soup when my son was sick. That is when I felt I was home."

Glasgow's future will be written by these newcomers as much as by its long-standing residents.

5.3.8 Conclusion: Migration as Glasgow's Lifeblood

Migration is not an episode in Glasgow's story. It is the plot. From famine ships to passenger jets, from Ellis Island dreams to asylum claims, the city's people have always arrived, adapted, resisted, and redefined what it means to belong.

In the kitchens of Pollokshields, the stairwells of the Gorbals, the prayer rooms of Govanhill, the dance halls of Dennistoun, **memory and migration intertwine**. Each arrival carries its own sadness and hope, and each has left a permanent mark on Glasgow's streets, syllables, and spirit.

To honour Glasgow's migrations is to embrace the complexity of identity, and to understand that this city's strength lies not in homogeneity, but in its ability to hold **many voices, many stories, and many homes**.

5.4 Women of Glasgow: Unheard Voices and Hidden Histories

5.4.1 Introduction: The City Through Her Eyes

Glasgow's history has long been told through the lens of shipbuilders, trade unionists, political leaders, and industrialists—figures most often male, muscular, and mythologised. But parallel to this dominant narrative runs another: one told in kitchens, streets, factories, schools, and soup kitchens. It is a **history of women**—working-class women, immigrant women, activists, carers, educators, artists, and mothers—whose contributions have too often been **unrecorded or undervalued**, yet whose fingerprints are all over the soul of the city.

This chapter seeks to **re-centre the lives and labours of women in Glasgow's story**, not as a supplementary footnote but as foundational to the city's past and future. It is a journey through resistance, care, creativity, and everyday resilience, spanning tenement doorsteps, picket lines, lecture halls, and community centres. These are not stories of passivity or silence, but of **agency, survival, and impact**—lived out beneath the weight of class inequality, patriarchal norms, and public invisibility.

Glasgow's women have **fought wars, built homes, fed families, raised protest banners, and carved space in boardrooms and boroughs**. Their histories, though often hidden, pulse beneath every sandstone street.

5.4.2 The Industrial Women: Toil and Tenement Life

In the 19th and early 20th centuries, as Glasgow expanded through industrialisation, its economic engine was not powered by men alone. Tens of thousands of women laboured in **textile mills, laundries, chemical plants, ropeworks, potteries, and domestic service**—earning low wages, enduring long hours, and juggling both economic work and the unpaid burden of child-rearing and housekeeping.

In the **jute mills of Partick** and the **textile works of Bridgeton**, women operated dangerous machinery, often losing fingers or developing respiratory diseases. Young girls started work at twelve or younger. In places like **Templeton's Carpet Factory**, housed in a lavish, Venetian-Gothic building, the grandeur of the facade belied the grim conditions inside.

Life at home in the tenements was no easier. With little plumbing, overcrowded rooms, and coal smoke thick in the air, **women bore the brunt of maintaining domestic life** in unhealthy environments. They stretched rations, shared washing greens, formed cooperative babysitting arrangements, and became the central pillar of community life. As one oral history puts it, "You could live on the fourth floor, but every wean on the stair knew whose mammy had a kettle on."

These women were not simply passive victims of poverty—they were organisers, survivors, and the first line of response in crisis.

5.4.3 Women of Protest: Rent Strikes, Picket Lines and Public Fury

Few moments in Glasgow's history show the power of working-class women more clearly than the **Glasgow Rent Strikes of 1915**, when tens of thousands of households refused to pay inflated rents during World War I. At the forefront were women like **Mary Barbour**, **Helen Crawfurd**, **Agnes Dollan**, and **Jean Ferguson**—part of the formidable "Mrs Barbour's Army."

These women:

- Organised **street-level resistance**, chased off bailiffs, and held mass meetings across Govan and Partick.
- Formed the **Glasgow Women's Housing Association**, which mobilised working-class women into political action.
- Secured a landmark legal victory: the **Rents and Mortgage Interest Restriction Act**, the first of its kind in Europe.

Later in the century, Glasgow's women continued to stand at the front of **labour disputes and community struggles**. In the 1970s, women were instrumental in the **Upper Clyde Shipbuilders' work-in**, feeding occupiers and sustaining morale. In the 1980s, they formed support groups during the **miners' strike**, often enduring arrest and surveillance themselves.

These were not "men's movements" with female supporters—they were, at many turns, **led and sustained by women.**

5.4.4 Mothers, Midwives and Moral Guardians: The Politics of Care

Women have always served as the city's **social glue**, holding together families, streets, and communities even as state support faltered. From the late 1800s, female nurses, midwives, and health visitors became central to Glasgow's public health infrastructure—though often with limited resources or formal recognition.

Figures like:

- **Dr. Marion Gilchrist**, Glasgow's first female medical graduate and a pioneer in women's health.
- **Mary Lily Walker**, a social reformer who highlighted infant mortality and poverty.
- Countless **midwives and "howdies"** who delivered babies in cramped tenements and soot-covered parlours.

In the 20th century, the emergence of **women's centres**—such as the **Castlemilk Women's Centre** or **Drumchapel Women's Aid**—provided critical support in areas where social services were absent or inadequate. These were spaces of **refuge, education, political organising, and healing**, particularly vital in combatting **domestic abuse**, which often went unreported and unpunished.

The ethic of care that ran through Glasgow's women was not merely personal—it was **radically political**, insisting that the everyday lives of the poor, the abused, and the excluded deserved dignity and protection.

5.4.5 Breaking the Silence: Gender, Race, and Intersectional Voices

Glasgow's feminist history cannot be understood without reckoning with **race, class, and immigration**. The story of women in the city is also the story of **South Asian women navigating patriarchal and racist structures, African and Caribbean women confronting exclusion**, and **Eastern European women building new lives as workers and mothers**.

Women like:

- **Asheikha Al-Khalili**, who advocated for Muslim women's rights within Scottish civic life.
- **Punam Kumar Gill**, a filmmaker and educator bridging South Asian and Scottish identity.
- **The women of Govanhill Baths Campaign**, where multi-ethnic, multi-faith collaboration created one of the most important grassroots movements in 21st-century Glasgow.

Intersectionality remains vital. The needs of a Polish domestic worker, a Roma mother, or a queer refugee woman are not always represented in traditional feminist spaces. Yet,

activists and artists are creating new narratives, weaving together migrant justice, LGBTQ+ advocacy, and working-class empowerment.

Modern groups like **Glasgow Women's Library**, **Ubuntu Women's Shelter**, and **Scottish Women's Aid** are working not only to preserve these voices, but to **amplify them into civic and cultural leadership**.

5.4.6 Culture, Creativity and Resistance: Women as Artists and Archivists

From the novels of **Alasdair Gray** to the murals of **St Mungo's**, Glasgow's culture often wears a masculine face. But beneath that façade lies a deep well of **female artistic expression**—often experimental, often radical, and deeply rooted in the social realities of the city.

Key figures include:

- **Liz Lochhead**, former Makar of Scotland, whose poetry and plays gave voice to working-class women and feminist consciousness.
- **Jackie Kay**, whose intersectional identity as a Black, gay, adopted woman from Glasgow shaped a generation of Scottish literature.

- **Hannah Frank**, a Jewish artist and sculptor whose work bridged romanticism and resistance.

The **Glasgow Women's Library**, the only accredited museum in the UK dedicated to women's history, holds thousands of archives chronicling lives that would otherwise vanish—letters, diaries, zines, protest leaflets, photographs, and oral histories.

Creativity has long been a weapon for Glasgow's women—not simply a form of escape, but of protest, preservation, and vision.

5.4.7 Conclusion: Rewriting the City in Her Name

To tell the story of Glasgow without its women is not just incomplete—it is inaccurate. The city as we know it has been forged through **female labour, pain, defiance, and imagination**. Whether on factory floors, in protest marches, behind closed doors, or in front of microphones, women have **shaped the pulse and pace of Glasgow**, generation after generation.

The task ahead is not just remembrance, but **reclamation**—to ensure that Glasgow's future honours not only the cranes and concrete but also the stories born in laundries, classrooms, kitchens, shelters, and song.

The next Glasgow will not simply be built by men with blueprints, but by **women with memories, ambitions, and refusal**—a city not just for her, but also shaped by her.

5.5 Activism and Action: From Red Clydeside to Climate Marches

5.5.1 Introduction: A City Born of Protest

Glasgow has always been more than brick and stone; it is a city animated by conviction, collective anger, and restless vision. From the cobbled streets of Govan to the halls of the City Chambers, from shipyards to school gates, Glasgow's civic identity has been moulded by **activism**—fierce, defiant, and often dangerous. It is not merely a city that endures hardship, but one that historically **organises against it**.

This chapter traces the evolution of Glasgow's protest culture, from the **revolutionary spirit of Red Clydeside** in the early 20th century to the **intersectional and climate-focused movements** of the 21st. At its heart lies a throughline of working-class solidarity, political consciousness, and the refusal to be ruled quietly. Whether fighting for housing, jobs, wages, gender rights, or the very future of the planet,

Glasgow's citizens have long recognised that **power rarely concedes without demand**.

5.5.2 Red Clydeside: Radicalism on the River

At the height of World War I, Glasgow became the epicentre of one of the most significant working-class uprisings in British history—**Red Clydeside**. The term refers not to a singular event but to a **sustained wave of radical, socialist, and labour activism** centred around the Clyde's industrial heartlands from 1910 to the 1930s.

Key moments and figures include:

- **1915 Rent Strikes** led by Mary Barbour and other working-class women in Govan, challenging landlords exploiting wartime housing shortages.
- **The 40-Hour Strike of 1919**, during which over **90,000 workers** protested for shorter working hours. The peaceful rally in George Square turned violent when police and military forces clashed with demonstrators—an event later dubbed **Bloody Friday**.
- Influential leaders such as **John Maclean**, a Marxist teacher and organiser imprisoned multiple times for his revolutionary politics; **James Maxton**, who

went on to lead the Independent Labour Party; and **William Gallacher**, future Communist MP for West Fife.

Red Clydeside wasn't just industrial unrest—it was **ideological transformation**, where working-class Glaswegians, inspired by socialism, trade unionism, and anti-imperialism, asserted their vision of a just society. Even though the revolutionary moment passed, its legacy remained etched in local memory, influencing political identities for generations.

5.5.3 Post-War Movements: From Urban Renewal to Civil Rights

In the post-World War II era, Glasgow faced mass demolition, dislocation, and reconstruction. Activism shifted focus to **housing rights**, **community autonomy**, and **civil equality**, often clashing with bureaucratic top-down planning.

Notable campaigns include:

- **The Gorbals Redevelopment Campaigns**, where residents resisted the wholesale demolition of tenements and fought for community input in rehousing schemes.

- **The Easterhouse Community Action Project**, formed in response to the alienation felt by those moved to peripheral housing estates with poor infrastructure and no social services.
- The rise of **anti-racist and immigrant advocacy** groups in the 1970s and 1980s, led by communities in **Pollokshields, Govanhill, and Maryhill**, who challenged police discrimination, workplace exclusion, and housing segregation.

Religious groups, women's organisations, and socialist coalitions began to intersect, giving rise to a **new kind of grassroots Glasgow**—one where **local knowledge, collective memory, and cultural identity** were used as tools of protest and preservation.

5.5.4 Women, Peace, and Power: Feminist and Anti-Nuclear Resistance

In parallel to labour and housing campaigns, Glasgow became a hub for **feminist activism**, especially during the 1970s and 1980s.

Key developments:

- The emergence of **Glasgow Women's Aid (1973)**, a pioneering institution supporting victims of domestic violence and reshaping public conversations about private abuse.
- The **Women's Peace Camp at Faslane**, just outside Glasgow, where for decades women protested the stationing of Trident nuclear submarines. Their vigils, sit-ins, and symbolic actions—such as weaving webs around fences—marked one of the most powerful visual statements against nuclear militarism in Scotland.
- The rise of **intersectional feminism**, particularly through the efforts of **South Asian, African, and Caribbean women**, who began organising against racism, patriarchy, and austerity.

Through these campaigns, women in Glasgow not only advocated for rights but **redefined the nature of activism**—infusing it with care, creativity, and inclusivity. Their work underscored that resistance could be both nurturing and confrontational.

5.5.5 Cultural Dissent and the Power of Art

Glasgow's activism has not been confined to petitions and picket lines. In the city's post-industrial era, **art, music, and performance** became powerful modes of dissent.

Examples include:

- **The Pollok Free State (1994–95):** An environmental and anti-road protest camp that blocked the construction of the M77 motorway through greenbelt land. Activists, artists, and local residents occupied woodlands, built treehouses, and created a micro-utopia that mixed protest with community building.
- **The GalGael Trust**, born from anti-road protests, using boatbuilding and traditional craftwork as a form of healing and resistance.
- **Glasgow's punk and indie music scenes**, which served as hotbeds for anti-Thatcher sentiment, anti-racism, and working-class expression, with bands like The Jesus and Mary Chain and Mogwai engaging politically through their sound and stance.

Murals across Glasgow—from George Floyd tributes to feminist banners on Bath Street—reveal how **the city walls have become protest platforms**, turning the urban environment into a living dialogue.

5.5.6 Climate, Youth, and the 21st-Century Movements

In recent years, Glasgow has seen a **new generation of activists emerge**, often led by youth, people of colour, LGBTQ+ communities, and climate justice organisers. These movements are deeply intersectional, recognising the **interconnectedness of economic, environmental, racial, and gender injustice**.

Milestones include:

- **School Strikes for Climate (Fridays for Future)**, led by Glasgow school pupils inspired by Greta Thunberg. Students marched through Buchanan Street and gathered at George Square demanding real action on emissions.
- **Extinction Rebellion Glasgow**, which staged die-ins, city centre road blockades, and performance protests, particularly targeting financial institutions and fossil fuel investors.
- **COP26 Protests (2021):** With Glasgow hosting the UN Climate Conference, over **100,000 people marched** through the city in one of the largest climate demonstrations in UK history. Indigenous leaders, youth strikers, unionists, and anti-colonial activists converged in an expression of global solidarity.
- Local campaigns such as **Stop the Pollok Park Development** and **Save the Southside Trees**, led by communities opposing overdevelopment and green space destruction.

What distinguishes 21st-century Glasgow activism is its **fluidity and hybridity**—it draws from local tradition while leveraging digital tools, global networks, and non-traditional tactics.

5.5.7 Conclusion: Glasgow as a Living Protest

From the **stormy banners of Red Clydeside to the urgent placards of climate strikes**, Glasgow's activism has never been ornamental—it has always been **necessary**. It is the heartbeat beneath public housing, the whisper behind every new mural, the anger that sharpens slogans, and the hope that assembles at dawn for another march.

The city's struggles are not relics of the past—they are evolving, intersectional, and as vital as ever. Glasgow is not just a place that remembers protest—it is a **place built by it**. Its resilience does not stem from passive endurance, but from a long-standing culture of **collective action and uncompromising solidarity**.

As the climate crisis intensifies, inequality deepens, and new political challenges emerge, Glasgow's protest tradition continues—louder, broader, and more imaginative than ever. In this way, Glasgow is still, and always will be, **a city in movement**.

Chapter 6: Glasgow's Hidden Layers – Lost Places, Secret Spaces

6.1 Underground Glasgow: Vaults, Tunnels, and Forgotten Foundations

6.1.1 Introduction: Beneath the Clyde, Beneath the City

Glasgow's history is not just inscribed in its grand façades or forgotten tenements. It is also buried—**literally**—beneath the ground. While the city above has modernised, risen, crumbled, and re-emerged over centuries, a **shadow city** has evolved below, a network of **tunnels, vaults, catacombs, and disused infrastructure**—each layer telling stories of enterprise, exploitation, fear, control, and curiosity.

Underground Glasgow is a city of silences and secrets, of darkened passageways that once pulsed with movement and machinery. It is where **Victorian engineers met medieval foundations**, where wartime bunkers met spiritual rites, where rumour and reality blend. This subterranean Glasgow is not just infrastructure—it is the hidden nervous system of a city shaped by trade, religion, empire, and resistance.

6.1.2 The Medieval Underlayers: Monks, Merchants and Burgh Walls

Beneath the modern sprawl of the East End and Merchant City lie remnants of **medieval Glasgow**. At the heart was the **cathedral precinct**, a spiritual and economic hub whose influence seeped underground as well as above.

- **Glasgow Cathedral's crypt**, dating to the 12th century, is one of the few fully intact medieval crypts in Scotland. It supported the cathedral's choir and housed the tomb of **St. Mungo**, Glasgow's patron saint. Still atmospheric and haunting, it was also used as a burial site for clergy and elite citizens.
- Nearby **Provand's Lordship**, the oldest surviving house in Glasgow (1471), hints at the layered nature of old Glasgow, built atop previous religious dwellings and trading posts.
- Beneath the High Street and Trongate were **early merchant cellars and tunnels**, allowing traders to store goods securely or transport them discreetly to the River Clyde.

Though less documented than later infrastructure, this medieval substratum reveals how **faith, commerce, and community** grew side by side—and how even early Glasgow was a city built in vertical layers, with the sacred and the secular coexisting in stone.

6.1.3 Victorian Vaults and Commercial Catacombs

The 19th century saw Glasgow explode into industrial greatness—and as it rose, it also burrowed. With population density soaring and new forms of commerce taking shape, Victorians engineered an **underground ecosystem** of vaults, basements, and private passageways to support the booming surface economy.

- **The Central Station Vaults**, perhaps Glasgow's most famous underground site, lie beneath one of the busiest railway terminals in the UK. This subterranean maze of red-bricked chambers, once used for coal deliveries, Victorian postal services, wartime sheltering, and secretive goods transfer, still gives guided tours. Stories abound of **workers crushed by falling stock**, **haunted shadows**, and **illicit late-night movements**.
- **Argyle Street Arches**—adjacent to Central Station—are a visible remnant of this vaulted world, converted into nightlife venues. But behind their trendy facades lie chambers once filled with **mechanical roar, human sweat, and grime**.
- **Merchant City** vaults and wine cellars remain locked away beneath restored townhouses and chic galleries. These were once used to store Caribbean rum,

Bordeaux claret, and later tobacco from Virginia—an eerie reminder of **Glasgow's links to empire and slavery**, hidden underfoot.

In these spaces, one feels the visceral tension between **economic ambition and human vulnerability**—industrial might built on invisible labour, its infrastructure disappearing into damp stone and dusty air.

6.1.4 Clyde Tunnel and Buried Infrastructure

As Glasgow modernised in the 20th century, its underground expanded from organic growth to **technocratic planning**. One of the most ambitious projects was the **Clyde Tunnel**, a pair of vehicular and pedestrian tunnels completed in 1963 to connect Whiteinch and Govan beneath the River Clyde.

- The construction required **pressurised tunnel boring**—a dangerous and pioneering method at the time. Workers known as **sandhogs** operated in high-pressure chambers to prevent river seepage. Many suffered from decompression sickness, or "the bends," as health protections were minimal.
- The pedestrian and cycle tunnels, still in use, have acquired urban legends of **ghosts, vanishing figures**, and inexplicable **lights flickering in otherwise abandoned corridors**.

Further infrastructure buried below includes:

- **Glasgow's disused railway tunnels**, such as the **Botanic Gardens Station Tunnel**, now home to graffiti artists, urban explorers, and foxes.
- Remnants of Glasgow's **early subway system**, opened in 1896, making it one of the world's oldest. Its circular loop remains functional, but older shafts and ventilation corridors lie dormant.
- **Victorian sewers**, especially those beneath **Kelvinbridge and Pollokshields**, built not just for waste but for rainwater control, now crumbling with age and mythologised for alleged **underground waterways** leading to secret exits from the city.

These structures reflect a shift—from religious sanctity and mercantile storage to **engineering spectacle and civil necessity**—each layer transforming Glasgow's relationship with what lies below.

6.1.5 War Bunkers, Cold War Shelters and Urban Myth

With the onset of the 20th century's global conflicts, Glasgow began to repurpose its underground as a **safety zone**. Its shipyards made it a bombing target, and its basements, tunnels, and bunkers became critical to the civilian war effort.

- **Air-raid shelters** were built under public parks like **Kelvingrove and Queen's Park,** and in school basements and residential blocks. Most are now sealed off, though traces remain—rusting ladders, steel doors, and disused ventilation shafts.
- **The Langside Bunker**, built during the Cold War in the 1960s, is an eerie subterranean complex once designated for emergency regional government. Its exact purpose is still partly classified, but it includes communication rooms, dormitories, and sealed chambers for "crisis continuity." Now decaying and flooded, it draws urban explorers intrigued by Cold War paranoia.
- Urban myths speak of **tunnels linking the University of Glasgow to Kelvingrove**, of **secret royal escape routes**, and of **Masonic passageways** beneath George Square—many unproven, but some plausible given the known scale of forgotten basements and utility conduits.

These spaces represent a **city bracing for collapse**, a place where survival required descent. They are haunted not by ghosts, but by the memory of **fear, resilience, and institutional secrecy**.

6.1.6 Myth, Memory, and Urban Exploration

In recent decades, Glasgow's underworld has attracted artists, researchers, and urban explorers drawn not just to the physical spaces but to their symbolism.

- Groups such as **Subterranea Britannica** and local "urbex" (urban exploration) communities have mapped and documented hidden sites—often entering illegally to capture the decaying elegance of Glasgow's abandoned tunnels.
- Photographers have published eerie portfolios of **moss-covered stairwells, rusting signage, flickering bulbs**, and flooded vaults beneath forgotten railway lines.
- Writers and artists have used these spaces to evoke themes of **forgotten history, economic decay, climate precarity**, and **psychogeography**—the emotional resonance of place.

What emerges is a sense that Glasgow's underground isn't just about infrastructure or mystery. It's a **repository of the city's subconscious**—the fears it suppresses, the eras it buries, the labour it forgets, the ambitions it outgrows.

6.1.7 Conclusion: A City Below the City

To walk through Glasgow today is to walk atop centuries of architecture, labour, resistance, empire, war, and myth. The tunnels beneath our feet carry no road signs, no GPS markers, yet they map an **entire emotional and social history**—a city carved into sandstone and soot, bearing witness in silence.

From medieval catacombs to Cold War bunkers, Victorian vaults to pedestrian tunnels, Glasgow's underlayers remind us that urban life is not only about the visible—it is also about the **obscured, the entombed, and the unfinished**.

As urban development threatens to seal or erase many of these sites, the need to **record, explore, and preserve** them becomes ever more urgent. For it is only by knowing what lies beneath that we can truly understand what stands above.

Glasgow, in this way, remains not just a city of layers, but a city of **echoes**.

Certainly. Below is **Chapter 6.2: Ghost Signs and Derelict Halls – Faded Echoes in the Urban Fabric**, written in the same extensive, detailed, and bulky format you've been using throughout the work.

6.2 Ghost Signs and Derelict Halls: Faded Echoes in the Urban Fabric

6.2.1 Introduction: Reading Between the Lines of a City

Every city has its silences. In Glasgow, these are often visible rather than audible: faded advertisements for long-defunct businesses on brick gables, soot-covered letters spelling out forgotten names, or the skeletal remains of grand public halls now boarded up or repurposed into supermarkets, car parks, or flats. These fragments—**ghost signs and derelict halls**—form a vernacular archive, a visual archaeology of commerce, community, and culture that refuses to be erased.

Unlike museums or monuments, these remnants are **accidental historians**. They survive in plain sight, uncurated, unprotected, yet full of meaning. Whether it's the barely legible lettering of a 1920s tobacconist or the crumbling pediment of a former Temperance Hall, such features whisper of **working-class lives, shifting moral landscapes, entertainment eras**, and **lost languages of trade and gathering**. They are Glasgow's memory made brick and mortar.

6.2.2 Ghost Signs: Typography, Trade and Time

Ghost signs—those faded hand-painted advertisements or shop names on the exteriors of old buildings—are more than nostalgic curiosities. They represent a layered commercial history stretching from the Victorian period to mid-20th-century Glasgow, a time when signage was painstakingly painted by hand and designed to endure.

Signage of Industry and Trade

Many ghost signs reflect Glasgow's **industrial heyday**, when even neighbourhood shops contributed to the vast supply chain of empire, coal, and manufacture.

- A faint "**A. M. Stevenson, Ironmonger**" sign on the Gallowgate speaks to the time when household goods, nails, and tools were all locally sourced, pre-supermarket and pre-global trade.
- In the Southside, remnants of "**James Dunn, Ship Chandlers and Marine Supplies**" still cling to a Pollokshields wall—residue of a business model tied to the Clyde's shipyards and a maritime culture now vanished.

Typography as Time Capsule

Each sign reflects a typographic fashion. Bold serif fonts from the late Victorian period. Elegant Art Deco scripts from the interwar years. Boxy sans-serif fonts from post-war Britain.

- The "**Co-Operative Bakery**" ghost sign on High Street, nearly invisible now, dates to an era when mutual aid and working-class organisation were not only economic models but physical landmarks.
- "**Players Please**" cigarette ads, once ubiquitous, still haunt pub walls in Partick and Springburn, a trace of the city's complex relationship with tobacco—from colonial import to local addiction.

The Persistence of the Painted Word

Ghost signs often survived demolition or rebranding because of their placement—**on side elevations**, above new shopfronts, or on upper stories left untouched by renovations. Time, pollution, and weather have turned them into **urban palimpsests**—where multiple eras coexist on a single wall.

Some have been intentionally preserved or restored, such as:

- The **George & Co. Tailors** sign in Garnethill, carefully repainted by a local artist collective.
- The **R.W. Forsyth** sign on Sauchiehall Street, protected during redevelopment efforts.

Each ghost sign is a **time-travelling document**, silently resisting the tide of urban erasure.

6.2.3 Derelict Halls: Spaces of Assembly and Abandonment

While ghost signs record commerce, **derelict halls** preserve a different kind of urban memory—one of **gathering, activism, morality, performance, and politics**. Glasgow was once teeming with public halls: **Temperance Halls, Working Men's Clubs, Mission Halls, Drill Halls, Orange Halls, and Music Halls**. These buildings served as the lungs of neighbourhoods, where people debated, danced, prayed, or agitated. Today, many lie empty or unrecognisable.

Temperance and Mission Halls

- **The Renfield Street Temperance Hall**, once the heart of Glasgow's anti-alcohol movement, hosted rallies, lectures, and social evenings promoting sobriety. Now demolished, its ideology survives in ghostly remnants: architectural fragments embedded into office buildings and archived pamphlets in Mitchell Library.
- In Govanhill and Calton, several **former mission halls** remain boarded up—once vibrant spaces where Christian groups offered free education, food, and

moral instruction to the urban poor. Their entrances, often adorned with **gospel quotations in stone**, are now choked by graffiti and moss.

Working-Class Assembly Spaces

- The **Shettleston Public Halls**, opened in 1903, were used for trade union meetings, suffragette talks, and musical performances. Deemed surplus to requirements in the 1980s, they now stand decaying, with local campaigns fighting for restoration.
- Many **Orange Halls**, still intact but underused, speak to the sectarian histories embedded in Glasgow's social structure. Their paint peels; their windows remain barred.

These spaces were once **neighbourhood anchors**, shaping identity through presence and participation. Their loss—through underfunding, arson, or redevelopment—reflects the broader disintegration of **communal public space**.

6.2.4 Lost Music Halls and Cinemas: Echoes of Entertainment

From the late 19th century to the mid-20th, Glasgow was often dubbed **"the second city of the music hall"**. Dozens of venues hosted comic acts, touring companies, operettas, and early film. Today, most are gone—some demolished, others awkwardly retrofitted into gyms, bingo halls, or flats.

Famous Names, Forgotten Sites

- The **Panopticon** on Argyle Street, where a teenage Stan Laurel performed, survives as a restored shell. Its exposed rafters and decaying curtains preserve a **ghostly ambience**, a kind of theatrical ruin-museum.
- The **Metropole Theatre**, beloved by working-class families for pantos and concerts, burned down in 1961. Its memory survives only in oral histories and family photo albums.

Art Deco Cinemas and Suburban Dreams

- The **Plaza Cinema** in Gorbals, with its sleek 1930s facade and neon signage, was once a Saturday institution for generations of Glaswegians. Closed in the 1980s, it was later flattened for housing developments.
- **The Riddrie Vogue** and **Kingsway Cinema** in Cathcart still stand, repurposed but retaining Art Deco features—curved glass, stepped cornices, deco lettering—evoking a glamorous past of **escapism and aspiration**.

For many, these were spaces of **first dates, childhood wonder, political awakening**, or musical discovery. Their gradual disappearance underscores a city moving from **communal spectacle to individual consumption**.

6.2.5 Community Memory and the Battle for Preservation

Despite their decayed state, both ghost signs and derelict halls **provoke memory** and invite public action.

- **Community campaigns** across the Southside and East End have tried to save old halls, proposing conversion into libraries, youth centres, or co-op housing.
- **Local artists and historians** document ghost signs photographically, publishing crowd-sourced maps and visual archives to capture them before they vanish under new paint or scaffolding.
- Some buildings—such as the **Govanhill Baths**—have been saved from demolition by grassroots efforts, transformed from ruins into community hubs.

What unites these efforts is a sense that these spaces and signs are not simply relics—they are **still alive**, still capable of **gathering meaning, memory, and people**.

6.2.6 Conclusion: Ephemeral Cities, Enduring Traces

Cities are not only built—they are **layered, overwritten, and revised**. Glasgow's ghost signs and derelict halls remind us that every street contains **multiple Glasgows**—the visible and the remembered, the vanished and the resurrected.

They challenge us to look harder at the margins, the in-between spaces, the cracks in the urban facade where history lingers in fading letters and crumbling cornices. They urge us to ask: what was here before? Who spoke, worked, gathered, and dreamed in this forgotten hall? What voices echo behind that faded painted word?

In a city often associated with resilience and reinvention, these echoes are not merely melancholic—they are signs of **continuity through change**. They remind us that while buildings fall and businesses close, **traces remain**. And those traces form the truest archive of what Glasgow was—and still is.

6.3 Urban Nature and Wild Corners: Green Pockets and Overgrown Stories

6.3.1 Introduction: Wildness at the Edge of Order

Glasgow has long prided itself on being a "Dear Green Place"—its name often interpreted from the Gaelic *Glaschu* as "green hollow." This identity is rooted not only in its 90+ public parks but also in something subtler, more enigmatic, and less officially mapped: the **urban wilds**—those tangled, overlooked, and uncultivated fragments of the city where nature, memory, and human neglect intersect.

From the unkempt edges of brownfield sites to overgrown railway embankments, community gardens sprouting between tenements, and rewilded factory lots now home to foxes and kestrels, Glasgow's **hidden green spaces** tell stories that landscaped gardens cannot. These are the sites where nature has not just been preserved, but where it has reclaimed space.

These wild corners are often seen as marginal or liminal—peripheral to the "main story" of Glasgow's urban narrative. But they are, in truth, **repositories of layered meaning**: environmental, historical, emotional, and social. These spaces also speak to

survival—not only of wildflowers and wildlife, but of communities, memories, and cultural improvisation.

6.3.2 Brownfield Beauty: Post-Industrial Wilderness

The **industrial heart of Glasgow** may have fallen silent in the late 20th century, but it left behind not only brick ruins and economic gaps—but ecological ones. Brownfield sites—vacant lots, derelict buildings, and former rail depots—have unintentionally birthed **urban meadows and forests**.

Take the **old St Rollox Railway Works** in Springburn. Once a site of roaring locomotives, it's now home to an accidental woodland where birch trees, rosebay willowherb, and wild grasses thrive. Pioneering species like buddleia colonize crumbling masonry, while insects, birds, and even deer pass through.

These places offer a **botanical archaeology**—wildflowers growing where oil drums once sat, moss carpeting machine bases, and saplings sprouting in the seams of red sandstone. For ecologists, these are vital **urban biodiversity hotspots**. For locals, they're secret gardens, play spaces, shortcuts home, or sources of foraged berries and apples.

6.3.3 Urban Wildlife: Foxes, Fungi, and Flight Paths

Wild Glasgow doesn't hide far. It's right there in the alley behind your flat, the wall at the bus stop blooming with ivy, the kestrel hovering over the M8 embankment, and the fox crossing Sauchiehall Street at dawn.

Red foxes, once limited to countryside dens, now raise their kits in backyard sheds and railway culverts. **Peregrine falcons** nest on brutalist tower blocks like the Red Road Flats once did. **Hedgehogs**, increasingly rare in rural environments, are often found in community gardens or along the Forth & Clyde Canal towpath.

Meanwhile, lesser-seen species—like **bats**, **rare mosses**, and **urban fungi**—have taken up residence in Glasgow's shaded groves and drain-pipe corridors. The city is threaded with hidden **green corridors**—unofficial pathways that connect fragmented habitats, allowing wildlife to move through concrete landscapes almost invisibly.

6.3.4 Secret Gardens and Community Oases

Amid tenement courtyards and vacant plots, **community gardens** have become sites of ecological activism, social gathering, and cross-cultural storytelling. Places like:

- **The Hidden Gardens** in Pollokshields—a contemplative space nestled behind the Tramway arts centre that fuses nature with multicultural identity.
- **Concrete Garden** in Possilpark—an urban farming collective growing vegetables, herbs, and flowers beside housing estates and high-rises.
- **South Seeds on the Southside**—a project helping residents turn neglected land into growing spaces, helping re-green the urban grid.

These gardens are not only green in the ecological sense—they're green in spirit: collaborative, hopeful, healing. They represent a **grassroots reweaving** of nature into the city, one raised bed at a time.

6.3.5 Ruins Reclaimed: Churches, Yards, and Factories

Glasgow's ruins tell stories long after their walls collapse. Many of these abandoned buildings—**burnt-out churches**, **old schoolyards**, **shipbuilding warehouses**—now sit quietly as hybrid landscapes.

St Peter's Seminary in Cardross, though outside Glasgow proper, exemplifies this phenomenon—a Brutalist ruin slowly being overtaken by nature, its chapel carpeted in moss, its staircases draped in vines.

Closer to the city, places like **Meadowbank Street** in the Gorbals reveal forgotten courtyards filled with birch trees that have seeded themselves in cracked cement. Walls crumble, but nature rebuilds—its architecture quieter, but enduring.

6.3.6 Rewilding in Plain Sight

Recent years have seen a push toward **intentional rewilding**, often led by local residents, artists, or environmental coalitions. Initiatives like the **Stalled Spaces program** have allowed unused land to be temporarily transformed into community greenspaces, sometimes with art installations, sometimes simply with seeds and hope.

Projects like **The Clyde Climate Forest**, launched in 2021, aim to plant millions of trees across Glasgow and the Clyde Valley region. These efforts acknowledge the

climate emergency but also a desire to return beauty, biodiversity, and carbon balance to urban life.

Even in everyday city infrastructure—green roofs, rain gardens, wildflower verges along new road builds—**a new aesthetic is emerging**, one that values messiness, diversity, and adaptability over Victorian neatness.

6.3.7 Emotional Landscapes: Memory and Refuge

These wild corners of Glasgow are also **emotional landscapes**—refuges of solitude, places of imagination, or sources of nostalgia. They appear in the work of Glaswegian poets, in schoolchildren's drawings, and in personal rituals—walking the dog, smoking in silence, or mourning a friend.

In areas undergoing redevelopment, there's often tension: between tidying up and preserving the **"feral beauty"** that offers comfort to so many. Many residents defend these spaces, not because they're pretty, but because they're **real**—they've grown organically, like communities themselves.

6.3.8 Conclusion: Nature, Not as Escape, But as Continuum

Urban nature in Glasgow is not separate from the city's story—it is an extension of it. These wild spaces are not interruptions, but **ongoing conversations**: between decay and regrowth, memory and possibility, constraint and freedom.

From the moss-stained foundations of vanished buildings to the sudden flutter of wings along the canal path, these green, gritty corners of the city offer more than beauty—they offer **truth, texture, and time**.

To walk through Glasgow's wild places is to walk through **layers of life**: natural, historical, and deeply human. And in doing so, you come to understand that the city's true heartbeat might just be found in the **hum of bees behind a bin shed**, the **whisper of grass on old railway tracks**, and the **roots pushing quietly beneath your feet**.

6.4 The City After Dark: Glasgow's Nighttime Narratives

6.4.1 Introduction: Shadows, Soundscapes, and Social Shifts

Nightfall in Glasgow is not merely a shift in the city's lighting—it is a **transformation of tone, mood, and meaning**. As the sun sets behind the gothic spires and high-rise flats, the city moves into another register. It is not just that the day ends; it's that a **different Glasgow begins**—one built not on productivity and commerce, but on rhythm, risk, ritual, and release.

The **Glasgow night** is many things at once: a stage for revelry, a canvas for neon-lit artistry, a backdrop for street-level survival, and a mirror reflecting the fractures of urban life. It is in the after-dark hours that the city's most haunting ghosts and liveliest characters appear. From the *throb of music echoing from basement venues* to the *silent glide of taxis crossing the Clyde*, night in Glasgow pulses with contrast and complexity.

The following narrative unpacks the hidden topographies of Glasgow's nocturnal life, traversing from dancefloors to doorsteps, from lamplit streets to lonely margins, capturing the city in its most **vulnerable, vibrant, and visceral** state.

6.4.2 After-Hours Architecture: Lighting, Landmarks and Liminality

The night reshapes the city's **physical identity**. Under sodium lamps, landmarks like the **University of Glasgow's cloisters**, the **City Chambers**, and the **Squinty Bridge** take on new character—glowing sentinels amid the darkness. **George Square** becomes eerie in its emptiness; **Central Station's clock** glows like a watchtower above still-busy streets.

But it's not just the showpiece structures that matter after dark. It's the alleyways behind **Sauchiehall Street**, the empty parking lots near **The Barras**, the tiled underpasses of **Charing Cross**. These are the **in-between places**, the urban thresholds that can feel either thrilling or threatening depending on who you are and how the city sees you.

Lighting itself becomes a **tool of control and expression**: festive in the Merchant City, functional in the East End, oppressive in housing estates. The night reveals **gaps in infrastructure**, but also allows for improvisation, where informal economies and street culture bloom in darkness.

6.4.3 Soundtrack of the City: Music, Movement and Memory

Glasgow's identity as a **music city** doesn't sleep. After dusk, it vibrates with sound—echoes of indie guitars, techno beats, traditional folk tunes, and hip-hop rhymes rising up from venues, clubs, and pub sessions.

Legendary spaces like:

- **King Tut's Wah Wah Hut** (where Oasis was famously discovered),
- **Sub Club** (a global destination for underground dance music),
- **The Barrowlands Ballroom** (a mythic venue pulsating with rock history),
- and newer hubs like **SWG3** and **BAaD** (in the Barras district)

anchor the nightlife landscape. These are not merely entertainment zones; they are **temples of communal experience**, sites of emotional release, creative experimentation, and scene-building.

Glasgow's music culture—raw, rebellious, and relentlessly DIY—spills out into the night. A busker on **Buchanan Street**, a ceilidh in a Southside hall, a grime freestyle in a car park—these sounds become **markers of identity and resilience**.

6.4.4 Pub Culture, Clubs, and Collective Rituals

From the warm wood-paneled pubs of the **West End** to the glitz of **Bath Street cocktail bars**, nightlife in Glasgow is also about **gathering, storytelling, and ritual**.

The pub remains the city's **true parliament**, where stories are shared, sorrows are soothed, and relationships begin or end. The late-night curry on **Byres Road**, the quiet pint in **Shawlands**, the chaotic singalong in **The Horseshoe Bar**—each moment tells part of the wider cultural narrative.

For younger generations and subcultural communities, **nightclubs** offer something more than hedonism. They are **spaces of identity formation**—for LGBTQ+ groups (like at **Polo Lounge** or **Delmonicas**), for ravers (at **La Cheetah**, **Berkeley Suite**), or for diaspora communities celebrating their own diasporic sounds.

But nightlife also has a **darker underbelly**. The fun can curdle into aggression. For some, especially women, people of color, queer folk, and disabled individuals, the night is not just a playground but a battleground. Safety, surveillance, and inclusion are contested constantly, with grassroots campaigns like **"Strut Safe"** and **"Girls Against"** working to reshape the narrative.

6.4.5 Night Shift: Workers and Watchers in the Margins

While some dance or drink, others work. Glasgow's nighttime economy relies on a network of often invisible labor: **bar staff, bouncers, taxi drivers, kebab shop workers, cleaners, police officers, and paramedics**.

- The **bouncer** navigating diplomacy and confrontation outside a packed venue.
- The **fast food worker** enduring rushes of chaos between 2 a.m. and 3 a.m.
- The **bus driver** running night services from the city to suburbs long after most people are asleep.
- The **NHS workers** on hospital night shifts, holding up lives in neon-lit corridors.

These workers experience a city that most others don't—a world of **late-night vulnerability**, altered states, and raw emotional outbursts. They often become **witnesses to society's contradictions**, from intimate confessions in cabs to violent encounters outside clubs.

6.4.6 Nocturnal Safety and Social Fragility

The night can be dangerous. It is in the darkness that **vulnerability intensifies**, especially for rough sleepers, those battling addiction, or young people with nowhere safe to go. While Glasgow is often a warm and welcoming city, it also grapples with **urban precarity**—and that's most visible after midnight.

Organizations like **Simon Community Scotland**, **Street Pastors**, and late-night outreach teams play a vital role, offering everything from warm drinks and blankets to harm reduction and mental health support. In the shadows of prosperity, Glasgow's night tells a story of **systemic gaps and human compassion**.

For women and marginalized people, walking home at night often involves careful calculation—of which street to take, what shoes to wear, how to hold your keys. Apps, safe zones, buddy systems, and education campaigns all seek to **reclaim the right to the night**, but structural change remains slow.

6.4.7 Sacred and Spiritual After Dusk

The night in Glasgow is also a time of **reflection and spirituality**. Churches like **St. Aloysius** or **Garnethill Synagogue** host evening services or vigils. Mosques in **Pollokshields** and **Govanhill** open for night prayers during Ramadan. At night, the quiet of faith becomes more pronounced, felt even in passing candlelight or a hush over community halls.

In modern secular Glasgow, other rituals have taken root: midnight yoga, full moon circles, grief groups, and queer-led ceremonies of healing and remembrance. These gatherings testify to a yearning for **connection, meaning, and comfort** in the night hours.

6.4.8 Ghosts, Myths, and the Paranormal

Night is fertile ground for the **supernatural Glasgow**—a city of haunted theatres, graveyard whispers, and ghost walks that traverse **The Necropolis, The Britannia Panopticon**, and **Provan Hall**.

Urban legends like the **Gorbals Vampire**, tales of **phantoms in the tunnels beneath Central Station**, and sightings in **Southern Necropolis** are not just spooky stories; they reflect deeper collective anxieties and cultural memories. These myths, passed down and remixed, become part of the **narrative architecture** of Glasgow's nights—stories that are told only when the lights go down.

6.4.9 Conclusion: The City That Dreams, The City That Remembers

Night is where Glasgow breathes differently. It is not merely a cessation of daylight, but a full reconfiguration of space, identity, and possibility. The same street can be joyous or threatening, depending on who you are. The same skyline that gleams by day becomes unknowable by night.

The **after-dark city** is where contradictions come alive: joy and sorrow, danger and connection, forgetting and remembering. It is a space of transformation—where day workers become dancers, where artists come alive, and where the city reveals not only what it is, but what it longs to be.

To understand Glasgow fully, one must walk it not only in the morning light, but in its **neon-lit midnights**, through fog, through laughter, through silence—where every story whispers a little louder when the rest of the city sleeps.

6.5 The Unseen City: Accessibility, Exclusion, and Inclusion

6.5.1 Introduction: Who Is Glasgow For?

At first glance, Glasgow presents itself as a city that welcomes everyone. Its humor, hospitality, and historical reputation for solidarity suggest inclusivity. But look closer—beyond the murals, the marketing, and the music—and another city emerges: one **not fully visible**, one in which **access is unequally distributed** and **exclusion quietly persists**.

Accessibility in Glasgow isn't just about **wheelchair ramps or braille signs**—though those are crucial. It's about **who feels they belong**, who gets to **shape the city**, who can **move through it freely and safely**, and who is **left navigating barriers**, both physical and social. The *unseen city* is the part of Glasgow that exists in **gaps, silences, and structural shortcomings**—where marginalised communities must improvise resilience in spaces not designed with them in mind.

This section explores how **accessibility, exclusion, and inclusion** intersect across the city, peeling back layers of inequality while also highlighting powerful stories of **community activism, adaptation, and hope**.

6.5.2 Mobility and the Built Environment: Navigating a Legacy

Glasgow is a city of hills, staircases, tight tenement closes, cobblestone lanes, and Victorian infrastructure. For many, this physical character is charming. For others—especially disabled people, older residents, and parents with prams—it is a **daily obstacle course**.

- **Subway stations**, built in the 19th century, are still largely inaccessible. Only a handful have lifts.
- Many iconic venues—**The Barrowlands, The Tenement House, King Tut's**—lack full step-free access or adequate disabled facilities.
- Pavement design varies wildly. Uneven kerbs, missing tactile paving, and narrow footways often force wheelchair users or blind pedestrians into traffic.

Accessibility advocates like **Glasgow Disability Alliance (GDA)** have fought tirelessly to raise awareness, offering training to planners and running community empowerment programs. Yet, many users still feel like **afterthoughts in the city's planning process**. The physical Glasgow remains shaped by decisions made generations ago—too often without consideration of mobility justice.

6.5.3 Invisible Barriers: Poverty, Class, and Urban Exclusion

Exclusion isn't always architectural—it's often economic. Glasgow's post-industrial geography has created **pockets of deprivation** where access to opportunity, safety, and leisure is limited by **postcode**.

- In districts like **Easterhouse, Drumchapel, Castlemilk**, and parts of **Govan and Possilpark**, public transport can be infrequent or expensive, jobs are scarce, and high-street regeneration rarely arrives.
- While the **West End and Merchant City** benefit from boutique shops and bustling cafes, other areas are **food deserts** or lack access to green space and libraries.

For many Glaswegians, the city feels **divided**, with certain zones seen as *off-limits*—economically, socially, or culturally. Class stigma lingers. A person's accent, address, or clothing can act as social shorthand, triggering subtle forms of **discrimination or distancing** in both public and private spaces.

Despite this, local groups and social enterprises have emerged in force:

- **GalGael Trust** in Govan fosters inclusion through traditional boatbuilding.
- **Kinning Park Complex**, once saved from closure by community occupation, now provides accessible space for grassroots action.

- **The People's Pantry** in Govanhill addresses food insecurity through solidarity rather than charity.

These efforts seek to **reclaim space and dignity** in places often overlooked by developers and policymakers.

6.5.4 Gendered Spaces and the Right to Feel Safe

Glasgow's public spaces can feel **fundamentally different depending on your gender**. While men may walk freely at night or occupy pub culture with ease, many women, non-binary people, and gender-diverse individuals experience the city through a lens of **risk assessment**.

- **Street harassment**, unwanted attention, and leering remain common. Certain routes—particularly underpasses, dimly lit parks, or alleyways—are avoided entirely.
- Transport hubs and late-night venues often lack **adequate safeguarding protocols** or staff trained to intervene when harassment occurs.
- The idea of a "normal route home" becomes fraught—what should be a basic urban right becomes a **navigational challenge of survival**.

Groups like **Strut Safe**, **Glasgow Girls Club**, and student-led campaigns have taken up the mantle of urban safety, advocating for better lighting, **safe walk apps**, and gender-aware planning. But broader cultural shifts—**educational, institutional, and systemic**—are needed for true inclusivity.

6.5.5 Language, Race, and Cultural Belonging

Glasgow's identity as a global city is more than academic—it's lived out every day in **Pollokshields**, **Govanhill**, **Maryhill**, and beyond. Yet, racialized Glaswegians still face **structural and interpersonal exclusions** that go beyond casual bias.

- **Language barriers** complicate access to healthcare, housing, and civic participation. English signage dominates public services, even in highly diverse districts.
- Racial profiling, **under-policing of hate crimes**, and **over-policing of youth of colour** remain real issues, particularly in schools and transport hubs.
- Urban design and heritage promotion often fail to reflect the **histories of Caribbean, Pakistani, Roma, African, Kurdish, Chinese, and Eastern European communities** that have shaped the city.

Projects like:

- **Africa in Motion Film Festival**,
- **Roma Cultural Festival**, and
- **The Colourful Heritage archive** (which documents the South Asian experience in Scotland)

are actively challenging these omissions by inserting **marginalised narratives into public consciousness**. These efforts create **alternative cartographies of belonging**, expanding the very definition of what Glasgow is—and who it's for.

6.5.6 Neurodiversity, Mental Health, and Sensory Inclusion

Accessibility also means **recognising invisible disabilities and neurodivergence**. From sensory-friendly hours in supermarkets to quiet rooms at public events, Glasgow has made some strides—but progress remains patchy.

- The city's **sensory overload**—flashing lights, traffic noise, crowded pavements—can be hostile to autistic people or those with PTSD or anxiety.
- Mental health services, while available, are often stretched thin. Long wait times and location-based gaps prevent equitable access.
- Young people navigating mental health challenges often encounter **bureaucratic walls**, while stigma still silences many adults.

Groups like **Voices of Experience (VOX)** and **See Me Scotland** are amplifying the voices of people with lived experience, pushing for **inclusive design that doesn't assume one norm**. Community centers are experimenting with quiet hours, art therapy sessions, and trauma-informed architecture.

The goal is not to create *separate spaces* but to make **all spaces welcoming to all minds and bodies**.

6.5.7 Faith, Belief, and the Right to Spiritual Space

Spiritual inclusion is another facet of the unseen city. Faith communities—Christian, Muslim, Hindu, Sikh, Jewish, Pagan, and secular humanist—often operate in the margins, adapting industrial buildings, community halls, or temporary facilities.

- **Mosques in Pollokshields**, gurdwaras in **Southside**, and synagogues in **Garnethill** offer both worship and welfare, but rarely feature in the city's design discourse.
- There are few **interfaith architectural spaces** or civic acknowledgements of the diversity of belief across the city.
- Pagan and spiritualist groups, while often robust, lack formal infrastructure.

Yet, in community gardens, solstice festivals, multi-faith vigils, and youth engagement programs, **new networks of spiritual solidarity** are quietly redefining how the sacred occupies space in a secular city.

6.5.8 Designing a More Inclusive Glasgow: Movements and Momentum

Glasgow's design legacy often reflects a **top-down approach**—post-war modernism, neoliberal regeneration, and spectacle-based urbanism. But this is slowly shifting.

From **participatory budgeting initiatives** to **community-led housing in Maryhill and Govanhill**, grassroots organisations are now insisting on being **co-authors of urban space**.

- **Civic House**, a refurbished 1920s print works in Cowcaddens, now hosts co-design labs and public engagement programs.
- **Glasgow Urban Lab** works across policy, planning, and academia to ensure lived experience is central to development.
- **Architecture & Design Scotland** has championed accessibility standards rooted in **universal design** rather than compliance minimalism.

Ultimately, inclusion requires **power redistribution**—designing *with*, not *for*—and centering the people often left out of the room.

6.5.9 Conclusion: Making the Invisible Visible

The unseen city is not truly invisible. It is only unseen if you're not looking. But the stories, struggles, adaptations, and advocacy that shape it are **vivid, vital, and deeply human**.

A truly accessible and inclusive Glasgow is not utopian—it is possible. It will be a city where:

- **A wheelchair user can board any bus or subway with ease.**
- **A queer Muslim teenager can walk down the street without fear.**
- **A neurodivergent artist can find space to create and connect.**
- **A working-class child from Possilpark feels as entitled to the city's beauty as anyone in the West End.**

Building this city means confronting past exclusions, amplifying unheard voices, and committing to **designing Glasgow not as a museum of past glories—but as a living, evolving home for everyone who calls it theirs**.

Chapter 7: Cultural Currents – Glasgow in the Arts and Imagination

7.1 On Screen and Stage: Glasgow in Film, TV, and Theatre

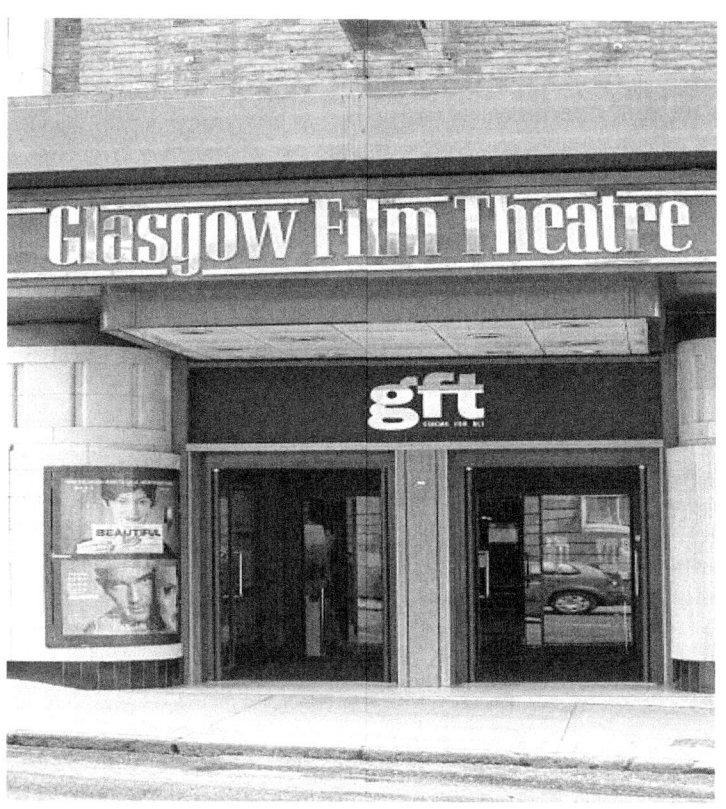

7.1.1 Introduction: A City Framed and Performed

Glasgow is a city that thrives on storytelling. In every corner of its built and natural environment, from soot-darkened sandstone to regenerated riverfronts, Glasgow holds a visual drama that demands to be captured, retold, and reimagined. It is not only a city with a vibrant arts scene—it is a city that becomes the art itself. On screen and on stage, Glasgow emerges as both a backdrop and a protagonist, standing in for other cities around the world or portraying itself with raw, unfiltered honesty.

This chapter explores the many ways in which Glasgow has been represented in film, television, and theatre. It examines how its locations, voices, and narratives have shaped— and been shaped by—media culture. It also considers how Glaswegian identity, with its distinctive working-class heritage, sense of irony, cultural pride, and history of political activism, has been projected globally through the performing arts.

7.1.2 Glasgow as a Filming Location: Doubles and Originals

Over the last two decades, Glasgow has become one of the most sought-after filming locations in the UK. Its diverse architecture—ranging from Victorian grandeur to post-industrial grit—makes it chameleonic, able to represent anywhere from 19th-century Paris to dystopian future cities.

Hollywood and Global Productions:

- *World War Z* (2013) famously transformed **George Square** and the surrounding Merchant City into downtown Philadelphia, with Brad Pitt fleeing a zombie apocalypse through familiar Glaswegian streets.
- *The Batman* and *The Flash* used **Glasgow Cathedral**, the **Necropolis**, and the **Gothic spires of the University of Glasgow** to evoke the brooding mood of Gotham City.
- *Indiana Jones and the Dial of Destiny* (2023) brought Harrison Ford to **St Vincent Street**, reimagined as 1960s New York, complete with vintage storefronts and yellow cabs.

TV Dramas and Series:

- Glasgow's own streets feature prominently in series such as *Shetland*, *Vigil*, and *Guilt*, even when the narrative is set elsewhere.
- The long-running *Taggart* (1983–2010) remains a foundational cultural artefact, portraying a gritty, crime-ridden Glasgow with a deadpan realism. The phrase "There's been a murder" became both meme and mantra, echoing across generations.
- *Still Game*, the cult comedy following two Glaswegian pensioners, uses local humour, dialect, and setting to reflect working-class life with affectionate satire.

Glasgow's appeal lies in more than just architecture. The city council's proactive Film Office offers streamlined permits and incentives, attracting productions that not only boost the economy but contribute to Glasgow's global image as a creative hub.

7.1.3 Glasgow on the Global Screen: Image and Identity

One of the more nuanced discussions in Glasgow's cinematic presence is how the city is portrayed when it plays itself. Unlike London or Edinburgh, which are often cast with a tourist gaze, Glasgow's on-screen identity tends to embrace its rough edges and complex contradictions.

Working-Class Realism: From Ken Loach's *Sweet Sixteen* (2002), shot in Greenock and Glasgow, to *Red Road* (2006), Andrea Arnold's haunting surveillance-driven drama set in the Red Road flats, filmmakers have often chosen Glasgow to explore themes of deprivation, alienation, and resilience.

Youth and Urban Culture:

- *Trainspotting* (1996), though famously associated with Edinburgh, used many interiors shot in Glasgow, including the **Crosslands Pub** in Maryhill.

- *Neds* (2010), Peter Mullan's semi-autobiographical depiction of 1970s gang culture in Glasgow, offered an uncompromising yet humanising look at inner-city masculinity, education, and violence.

Modern Reimaginings: Recent projects have aimed to showcase a broader image of the city—one that includes **multiculturalism**, **creativity**, and **social change**. Films and documentaries exploring South Asian, African, and Eastern European communities in Govanhill and Pollokshields are shifting the narrative toward one of diversity and inclusion.

7.1.4 Glasgow's Theatre Scene: From Oran Mor to the Citizens

While screen productions reach global audiences, Glasgow's **theatre scene** has long served as the city's cultural conscience. From classical Shakespearean productions to radical contemporary performance, Glasgow's stages speak in many voices.

The Citizens Theatre (The Citz): Founded in 1943, "The Citz" has a legendary reputation for staging bold, socially-engaged work. Located in the Gorbals, its very position is symbolic—a beacon of high art in a historically working-class neighbourhood. Over the decades, it has nurtured talents like Rupert Everett, Alan Rickman, and David Hayman, while developing daring reinterpretations of Brecht, Beckett, and Scottish classics.

Tron Theatre: Situated in the Merchant City, the Tron combines a historic building with progressive programming. It supports new writing and experimental works, including collaborations with playwrights exploring LGBTQ+, postcolonial, and neurodivergent themes.

Oran Mór and A Play, A Pie, and A Pint: One of Glasgow's most distinctive contributions to contemporary theatre is this lunchtime tradition. Founded by David MacLennan, it offers accessible, affordable theatre in a casual setting—breaking down the perceived elitism of stage performance and introducing new talent weekly. It exemplifies Glasgow's democratic approach to the arts: no hierarchy, no barriers, just stories well told.

National Theatre of Scotland: Though not headquartered in a fixed venue, the NTS is deeply rooted in Glasgow's artistic ecosystem. It often partners with venues like Tramway, The Arches, and the Citz, bringing bold, mobile productions to unconventional spaces—including warehouses, forests, and even ferries.

7.1.5 The Sound of the City: Music and Performance in Narrative

Film and theatre in Glasgow are deeply interwoven with music, another foundational element of the city's identity. Whether in the live scoring of silent films at the **Glasgow Film Festival**, the use of local bands in contemporary soundtracks, or musicals like *Sunshine on Leith* that channel the spirit of Scottish working-class optimism, the city pulses with rhythm.

The **Barrowland Ballroom** appears in countless documentaries and dramas, often symbolising a kind of sacred space for the working-class Glaswegian soul. Artists from Franz Ferdinand to Mogwai to Lizzie Reid have contributed to a sonic landscape that merges with visual storytelling to give Glasgow its distinct media identity.

7.1.6 Conclusion: The Performance of a City

Glasgow on screen and stage is never just a location—it is an active, living presence. Whether doubled for New York or standing proudly as itself, it holds within it contradictions and complexities that demand artistic exploration. It is gritty and grand, humorous and haunted, scarred and soulful.

The power of performance in Glasgow lies not only in its visual possibilities but in its people: actors, writers, technicians, storytellers, and audiences who know the value of a good narrative and the necessity of telling it well. As global platforms continue to amplify Glaswegian voices and settings, the city remains one of the world's most compelling cultural protagonists—endlessly watchable, deeply human, and defiantly unique.

7.2 The Music Walk: Venues, Voices, and Vibrations

7.2.1 Introduction: The Pulse of a City

Few cities wear music as proudly—and as deeply—as Glasgow. In the streets of the city centre, in converted warehouses and aging church halls, in the laneways of the West End and the clubs of the Southside, music is not just entertainment; it is identity, resistance, memory, and movement.

Designated a UNESCO City of Music in 2008, Glasgow's global musical status is not defined by a single genre or scene. Instead, it thrives in layers—punk and pop, indie and folk, techno and trad, all vibrating against the city's tenements, concert halls, and cobbled alleys. To walk through Glasgow is to walk through sound, and this chapter traces that walk: from iconic venues to legendary artists, from street buskers to international headliners.

7.2.2 The Venues: Temples of Sound

Glasgow's live music venues are more than spaces—they are institutions, with decades of cultural memory embedded in their walls.

Barrowland Ballroom (The Barrowlands):
 If Glasgow has a musical heart, it beats inside the neon glow of the Barrowlands. Originally opened in 1934 and rebuilt in 1960, this iconic venue in the East End has hosted legends—from David Bowie and Simple Minds to The Smiths, Oasis, and Amy Winehouse. With its sprung wooden dancefloor and celestial ceiling lights, it remains both sacred ground for fans and a rite of passage for performers. To "sell out the Barras" is to earn Glasgow's blessing.

King Tut's Wah Wah Hut:
 Small in size but colossal in influence, King Tut's on St. Vincent Street is forever etched into music lore for "discovering" Oasis in 1993. But that's just the beginning. This 300-capacity venue has been a launching pad for acts like Radiohead, The Killers, Florence + The Machine, and Paolo Nutini. Its intimate size brings fans within sweat's reach of performers, creating the perfect alchemy for breakout moments.

The Hydro & SEC Armadillo:
At the other end of the spectrum lies the Hydro—a gleaming, futuristic arena with a capacity of over 14,000. Opened in 2013, it has cemented Glasgow's status as a global tour stop for artists like Beyoncé, Elton John, Billie Eilish, and Lewis Capaldi. Adjacent, the Armadillo (Clyde Auditorium) hosts more formal, seated performances—from symphonic rock to classical orchestras and spoken word.

Other Notables:

- **The Garage** and **Cathouse**: staples of the rock and alternative scene.
- **Mono**, **Nice N Sleazy**, and **Broadcast**: venues that double as cultural hubs for independent and experimental acts.
- **The Old Fruitmarket**: a beautifully restored market hall in the Merchant City, now hosting folk, jazz, and world music.
- **SWG3**: a multidisciplinary arts complex in Finnieston, housing club nights, raves, and art installations. A symbol of Glasgow's genre-fluid future.

7.2.3 The Artists: From City Streets to World Stages

Glasgow's music scene has long been characterised by its DIY ethic, its political edge, and its emotional sincerity. Its artists are storytellers, provocateurs, poets—and they reflect the city's tensions and triumphs.

1980s–1990s: Pop, Post-Punk and Indie Explosion

- **Simple Minds** and **Hue and Cry** brought Glaswegian sounds to the pop charts, balancing social commentary with stadium-friendly choruses.
- **The Jesus and Mary Chain** and **Primal Scream** emerged from the post-punk underground, fusing noise, rebellion, and dance into cult classics.
- **Belle and Sebastian**, perhaps the quintessential Glasgow indie band, defined a generation with their literate lyrics and delicate melodies. Their rise from university gigs to global acclaim represents the power of Glasgow's small venues and fanzine culture.

2000s–2010s: Eclecticism and International Reach

- **Franz Ferdinand** spearheaded a new wave of guitar-led dance rock, winning Mercury and Brit awards while staying rooted in local rehearsal spaces and design schools.
- **Chvrches**, the synth-pop trio from Glasgow, brought electronic melancholy to international audiences, blending emotional honesty with stadium-ready hooks.
- **Paolo Nutini**, born in Paisley but raised on Glasgow's musical currents, became a soulful voice of a new Scotland, mixing blues, folk, and pop.

Contemporary Voices:

- **Joesef**, hailing from the East End, brings queer identity and neo-soul together with cinematic elegance.
- **Lizzie Reid**, **The Ninth Wave**, and **Walt Disco** represent a new generation that is genre-blurring, emotionally raw, and proudly progressive.
- Glasgow's rap and grime scene—less mainstream but increasingly vital—is finding its voice in artists like **Bemz**, **Washington**, and **Nova**.

7.2.4 Local Legends and Lifers: The Unseen Backbone

Beyond the charts and tours lies the network of lifers—the pub musicians, community choir leaders, rehearsal studio owners, and record store clerks—who keep Glasgow's scene alive.

- **Tam Coyle**, a long-time promoter and DJ, is often cited as a quiet kingmaker behind dozens of local successes.
- The folk sessions at places like **The Ben Nevis** and **The Scotia Bar** connect generations through oral tradition and string instruments.
- Glasgow's community radio stations—especially **Clyde Built Radio** and **Subcity**—serve as cultural transmitters, amplifying underground artists and niche genres.

7.2.5 Music as Protest and Power

Glasgow's music has often been entwined with resistance. From anti-Thatcher punk to pro-independence anthems, from queer club nights that offer safe space to songs that mourn lost industries and rising rents, the city sings what it cannot be allowed to say.

- **Red Clydeside folk music** once chronicled labour strikes and tenant marches.
- **Protest singers** like **Dick Gaughan** and **Karine Polwart** carried those themes into modern movements.
- **Club nights like Shoot Your Shot and Missing Persons Club** are not only sonic adventures—they are affirmations of queer identity, anti-capitalist joy, and radical love.

7.2.6 Glasgow's Sonic Ecosystem: Labels, Studios and Education

- **Chemikal Underground Records**, founded by The Delgados, is one of Scotland's most influential indie labels, fostering talent like Mogwai and Arab Strap.
- **Green Door Studio** and **La Chunky** are havens for analog experimentation, nurturing lo-fi creativity in the digital age.

- Institutions like the **Royal Conservatoire of Scotland** and **Glasgow School of Art** act as incubators for talent, often blurring the lines between classical training and contemporary disruption.

Record stores like **Love Music**, **Rubadub**, and **Mixed Up Records** continue to thrive, serving as both retail spaces and meeting points for Glasgow's audiophiles and crate diggers.

7.2.7 The Soundtrack of the Streets: Informal Scenes and Everyday Music

It's not just the big names or big venues that define Glasgow's music. The buskers on **Buchanan Street**, the drum circles in **Kelvingrove Park**, the gospel choirs in **Pollokshields**, and the tabla rhythms from open windows in Govanhill all contribute to a living, breathing sonic landscape.

Music is heard in council flats and converted mansions, in late-night kebab shops and on rush-hour trains. It's performed in Gaelic and Urdu, in sign language and verse, with fiddles or laptops. The city is both stage and studio, always in rehearsal for something beautiful.

7.2.8 Conclusion: A City in Song

Glasgow doesn't just make music—it **is** music. Every bar, every chant, every beat resonates with the city's lived experiences: the grind of the shipyards, the energy of the dancefloor, the ache of longing, the thrill of defiance.

Its music scene is neither fixed nor finished. It shifts with each generation, opening new doors while honouring old ones. Whether you're in a sweat-drenched basement venue, a soaring concert hall, or walking the quiet towpaths of the Clyde with headphones on, Glasgow's vibrations stay with you—urgent, tender, wild, and true.

7.3 Street Art and Graffiti: Walls That Speak

7.3.1 Introduction: Glasgow's Living Canvas

In Glasgow, the streets don't just carry footsteps—they speak. The city's walls, alleys, bridges, and shuttered shopfronts have evolved into a vast open-air gallery, a democratic canvas where local voices, global influences, political defiance, and sheer creative joy erupt in pigment, paste, and spray. Street art and graffiti in Glasgow are not just adornments or subcultural tags; they are layered conversations—sometimes loud, sometimes whispered—between the city and its people.

Glasgow's artistic soul has always existed outside traditional institutions. While its galleries and art schools have produced world-renowned talent, it's the public realm—the uncurated, unsanctioned, and often ephemeral art in the streets—that offers the most honest expression of the city's psyche. Here, graffiti and street art aren't opposites but overlapping traditions: graffiti as rooted in tagging and identity-marking; street art as visual storytelling, muralism, and sometimes protest.

7.3.2 A Short History of Glasgow's Graffiti and Street Art Scene

The Early Years: Tagging, Turf, and Rebellion (1980s–1990s)

Glasgow's early graffiti culture was born alongside the social discontent and urban decay of the late 20th century. As industries declined and public investment shrank, walls became battlegrounds of youth expression. Tags, throw-ups, and political slogans began appearing across rail yards, underpasses, and derelict buildings, often dismissed by authorities as mere vandalism.

This was a time when graffiti was about **territory and voice**—a way for working-class and often marginalized youth to claim space in a city that was quick to overlook them. Crews like **TDS** and **FGA** marked out their zones in coded acronyms and bold fonts. These early writers were heavily influenced by the transatlantic currents of New York-style graffiti, filtered through Glasgow's own gritty realism.

2000s–2010s: Street Art Emerges, Murals Multiply

By the early 2000s, Glasgow began to experience a shift. While graffiti persisted underground, street art—especially large-scale murals and stencil work—began to gain institutional recognition and civic support. This was in part catalyzed by regeneration projects and tourism strategies, but also by artists pushing for the street as a valid canvas for visual culture.

One pivotal moment was the launch of **The City Centre Mural Trail** in 2014, a council-supported initiative that commissioned artists to paint large-scale works across neglected or blank urban surfaces. While some in the graffiti community saw this as co-option, the murals undeniably transformed parts of the city into vibrant, visually arresting environments—and helped legitimize public art as a tool of cultural storytelling.

7.3.3 The Mural Trail: Glasgow's Official Open-Air Gallery

The **Glasgow City Centre Mural Trail** includes over 25 murals stretching across Trongate, Merchant City, and the riverside. Though "official," many of these murals are anything but sanitized. They are bold, intricate, and politically resonant.

Some standout works include:

- **"Fellow Glasgow Residents" by Smug (Sam Bates):**
  This hyperrealist masterpiece stretches across an entire gable end on Ingram Street. It features various animals native to Scotland—foxes, deer, squirrels—blended with urban architecture, highlighting the fragile coexistence of nature and city.

- **"St. Mungo" by Smug:**
  Perhaps the most iconic mural in Glasgow, this reinterpretation of the city's patron saint shows a contemporary, hoodie-wearing young man tenderly holding a robin. It reclaims a religious figure into modern working-class imagery, subtly challenging traditional narratives.

- **"The World's Most Economical Taxi" by Rogue-One (Bobby McNamara):**
  A visual joke featuring a man in a shopping trolley hurtling down a hill, this piece on Mitchell Street fuses Glasgow's sharp wit with kinetic energy.

- **"The Clutha Vaults Tribute" by Rogue-One and Ejek:**
  Painted on the side of the pub tragically hit by a police helicopter in 2013, this

mural memorializes lost lives and celebrates the role of the Clutha in Glasgow's live music scene.

These murals don't just beautify—they localize. They bring forgotten walls into the realm of memory and meaning, telling stories of workers, musicians, wildlife, and ordinary Glaswegians often erased from more formal records.

7.3.4 Graffiti: The Wild Voice of the City

Outside of the mural trail and sanctioned artworks, **graffiti continues to thrive**—raw, fast, and politically charged. Walk through the underpasses near **Partick**, the abandoned buildings of **Govan**, or the tunnel systems under **Central Station**, and you'll find a different aesthetic: layered, chaotic, and rebellious.

Graffiti in Glasgow is not homogenous. Some pieces are elaborate burners, done by artists with years of technical skill and coded reputations. Others are scrawled messages in marker or stickers slapped onto street signs and phone boxes. But all operate within a **code of immediacy**, a sense that this might not be here tomorrow—and that it was made not for tourists, but for those who truly walk the city.

Political graffiti plays a vital role in Glasgow's street language:

- Anti-Tory, pro-independence slogans.
- Support for Palestine and critiques of colonialism.
- Anti-police messages, especially after publicized incidents of immigration raids in areas like Pollokshields.
- Feminist and queer affirmations scrawled on pub toilets and lampposts.

There are also **graffiti festivals** and legal walls, like those supported by the **Yardworks project at SWG3**, where international and local artists collaborate on massive pieces in rotating exhibitions. Yardworks offers a rare point of convergence: where graffiti, street art, and hip-hop culture can meet the public without dilution.

7.3.5 Female and Queer Street Artists: Reclaiming the Walls

Street art has historically been male-dominated, but Glasgow's newer wave is increasingly shaped by women and LGBTQ+ artists using walls as platforms for identity and inclusion.

- **Ejek**, **Mikaela Gallacher**, and **KMG** are among the rising artists creating works that disrupt gender norms and celebrate underrepresented bodies.
- The **"Free Period Scotland" mural** (2019) tackled period poverty with vibrant, unapologetic imagery—sparking conversations and headlines.

- Murals in Govanhill have celebrated immigrant communities, queer pride, and solidarity with trans rights, reflecting the area's global diversity and progressive ethos.

These murals aren't just visual—they're activist. They force questions. Who owns public space? Whose voices deserve to be seen?

7.3.6 Street Art Tours and Community Projects

Walking tours have grown in popularity as a way to explore Glasgow's street art. Companies like **Walking Tours in Glasgow** and **Glasgow Street Art Tours** don't just show the works—they explain the politics, the backstories, the tensions between legal and illegal, the quiet erasures and proud declarations.

Community murals have also flourished in:

- **Easterhouse** and **Drumchapel**, where public art projects work with local youth to challenge stigma.
- **Govan's "We Are Still Here"** project, which foregrounds working-class history and resilience.
- **Pollokshields Arts Collective**, known for popup murals and projections supporting refugee rights and community defence.

Here, art becomes resistance, therapy, and collaboration.

7.3.7 The Future of the Street: Challenges and Questions

As Glasgow continues to evolve, so too does its relationship with public art. Questions persist:

- Can street art remain radical if it becomes too curated?
- What happens when graffiti is criminalized but murals are funded?
- Is there space for both expression and preservation?

Some fear that the success of the mural trail has led to gentrification—a sanitised version of street culture divorced from its grassroots. Others see it as a bridge: a way to introduce street aesthetics to broader audiences, while underground graffiti maintains its raw edges in the shadows.

The **best future**, perhaps, lies in tension: a city where legal and illegal coexist, where public art is both celebration and challenge, where walls are still free enough to speak.

7.3.8 Conclusion: The City Writes Back

In Glasgow, art is not confined to frames—it spills onto bricks, shutters, railings, and rooftops. Its messages are layered, transient, sometimes contradictory—but always alive. The city's walls are diaries, protests, love letters, warnings, and declarations of presence.

Whether it's a hyper-detailed mural downtown, a hastily scrawled tag in Maryhill, or a wheatpaste poster announcing resistance in Govanhill, **Glasgow's walls do not whisper—they shout, they sing, they remember**.

The city writes itself every day—and the story is never finished.

7.4 Glasgow in Literature: From Alasdair Gray to Modern Memoir

7.4.1 Introduction: A City Written from the Inside Out

Glasgow has long been a city of words as much as one of work, politics, or song. Its literature is not an ornamental afterthought—it is integral to how the city has defined, questioned, and remade itself. While Edinburgh may claim the moniker of "City of Literature," Glasgow's literary voice is less manicured, more visceral—a product of class consciousness, political urgency, linguistic richness, and the grit of everyday life.

Writers here don't just write about the city; they write **from it**. Glasgow is not merely a setting—it is a **character**, a language, a wound, and a chorus. From Alasdair Gray's mythic realism to James Kelman's defiant working-class interiority, from Liz Lochhead's lyrical dialects to the recent surge in memoir and autofiction, Glasgow's literary imagination is vast, diverse, and persistently grounded in place.

7.4.2 Alasdair Gray: Architect of an Imagined City

No discussion of Glasgow in literature can begin without **Alasdair Gray**. His seminal novel *Lanark: A Life in Four Books* (1981) is not only a landmark in Scottish literature—it's a rewriting of Glasgow into an allegorical, dystopian, yet deeply personal mythscape.

Gray transforms Glasgow into **Unthank**, a surreal, oppressive city that is both utterly recognizable and maddeningly abstract. Through a fractured narrative that blends realism, science fiction, autobiography, and metafiction, *Lanark* presents the city as a psychological labyrinth—wounded by industrial decline, authoritarian bureaucracy, and emotional alienation.

Gray, a visual artist as well as a writer, saw Glasgow not only as a city to describe but to **draw, paint, and reconstruct**. His typography, marginalia, and visual maps of the city reflect a total aesthetic—a city reimagined as both canvas and text. His other works, including *1982, Janine* and *Poor Things*, continue to interrogate power, sexuality, and memory, all through a Glaswegian lens.

7.4.3 James Kelman and the Raw Voice of the Working Class

Where Gray's language was expansive and playful, **James Kelman** brought radical minimalism and authenticity. His Booker Prize-winning novel *How Late It Was, How Late* (1994) follows Sammy, a working-class Glaswegian ex-con, as he navigates blindness and existential isolation. It is written in a stream-of-consciousness Glaswegian vernacular that shook the literary establishment and earned both acclaim and controversy.

Kelman's prose is fierce, unsentimental, and profoundly political. By writing in demotic Glaswegian, he refused the conventions of standardized literary English, asserting that **working-class Scots speech was worthy of serious literary treatment**. This was more than a stylistic choice—it was a philosophical stance against cultural erasure and linguistic imperialism.

Kelman's other works, such as *The Busconductor Hines* and *A Disaffection*, similarly centre on **ordinary lives rendered extraordinary** through intimate, fragmented internal monologue. Glasgow in Kelman's work is not romanticized—it is indifferent, harsh, yet capable of fleeting grace and humour.

7.4.4 Janice Galloway, A.L. Kennedy, and Literary Intimacies

While Kelman and Gray often worked in panoramic or polemic modes, writers like **Janice Galloway** and **A.L. Kennedy** have honed more intimate narratives of identity, trauma, and the psychology of Glaswegian life—especially through female perspectives.

Galloway's *The Trick Is to Keep Breathing* (1989) explores a young woman's descent into grief and mental illness, set against a backdrop of suburban Glasgow and oppressive social norms. Her use of fragmented structure, typographic experimentation, and inner dialogue owes much to modernist traditions but is also fiercely Glaswegian in tone.

A.L. Kennedy, though often ranging beyond Glasgow geographically, brings a dark wit and emotional intensity to her portrayals of alienation, failed intimacy, and spiritual dislocation. Her Glaswegian characters are rarely stereotypes—they are complex, wounded, and trying to love despite themselves.

7.4.5 Memoir, Memory, and Margins: The Rise of Personal Glasgow

The past two decades have seen a resurgence in **memoir and autofiction**, often from writers of marginalized backgrounds reclaiming space in the city's literary history.

- **Douglas Stuart's *Shuggie Bain*** (2020), winner of the Booker Prize, is perhaps the most internationally lauded recent example. Set in Thatcher-era Glasgow, it chronicles a young boy's coming-of-age as the son of an alcoholic mother. Stuart, writing from New York, reanimates 1980s working-class Glasgow with aching tenderness, dialectal authenticity, and unflinching detail. The novel is as much about addiction and resilience as it is about **queer survival in a city that offered little room for difference**.

- **Chitra Ramaswamy**, in her hybrid memoir *Expecting* and collaborative work *The Full Scottish Breakfast*, brings diasporic and intergenerational memory into the foreground, exploring what it means to be a brown Scottish woman in a city still reckoning with its colonial entanglements.

- **Denise Mina**, a writer of both fiction and nonfiction, uses Glasgow as the canvas for crime, justice, and gender politics. Her novels, including the *Paddy Meehan* and *Alex Morrow* series, peel back the facades of Glasgow's institutions to reveal the racism, corruption, and class inequalities within.

7.4.6 Glasgow's Poets: Dialect, Protest, and the Lyrical City

Glasgow's literary life is not confined to prose. Its **poetic traditions** are rich and diverse, rooted in dialect, performance, and political engagement.

- **Liz Lochhead**, former Scots Makar and proud Glaswegian, fuses Scots dialect with feminist insight and humour. Her performances, often given in cabaret and theatrical settings, blur the line between poet and playwright.

- **Tom Leonard**, a peer and intellectual ally of Kelman, famously challenged language hierarchies in poems like *"Unrelated Incidents"*, where the Glaswegian accent is central to the poem's resistance. His work interrogated who gets to speak and whose voice is considered "literary."

- **Jackie Kay**, former Makar and adopted Glaswegian, writes deeply human poems on identity, adoption, race, and queerness, often filtered through Glasgow's multicultural textures.

- In recent years, **spoken word collectives** like **Sonnet Youth** and **Loud Poets** have brought poetry to bars, clubs, and social media, creating a vibrant new scene that blends lyricism with social critique.

7.4.7 Libraries, Bookshops, and Literary Infrastructure

The literary heartbeat of Glasgow also pulses through its public spaces:

- **The Mitchell Library**, one of Europe's largest public libraries, has served as a literary sanctuary for over a century. It is both a place of study and a democratic temple of reading.

- **Bookshops like Aye-Aye Books, Category Is Books** (Scotland's first queer bookshop), and **Calton Books** (focusing on leftist and working-class literature) contribute to a literary ecosystem that is as political as it is creative.

- Events like **Aye Write!**, **Outwith Festival**, and **Wee Write** draw diverse audiences into dialogues about literature, class, gender, migration, and identity.

7.4.8 Conclusion: The Never-Ending Story of a City

Glasgow is not one literary city—it is many. It is a site of invention, resistance, tenderness, and reinvention. From Gray's sprawling metafictions to Stuart's intimate elegies, from spoken word nights in bars to the quiet aisles of the Mitchell Library, literature in Glasgow is not confined—it **breathes**, it **fights**, and it **remembers**.

To read Glasgow's literature is to enter into **an ongoing conversation**—between past and present, between form and feeling, between the personal and the political. It is a city that does not ask for permission to speak—it writes because it must. And its stories, fierce and fragile, are still unfolding.

7.5 Museums, Galleries and DIY Spaces: Curating the City

7.5.1 Introduction: A City Curated by Its People

Glasgow is a city where culture is not imposed from above, but rather **curated from within**—in galleries and museums, yes, but also in squats, shipping containers, church halls, and repurposed factories. The city's identity is deeply bound up in the visual arts—not only in its celebration of internationally recognized works but also in the flourishing of grassroots initiatives and experimental spaces.

With a reputation as Scotland's creative powerhouse, Glasgow has consistently produced and nurtured artists who challenge, provoke, and reimagine. Its world-class institutions stand beside a restless and ever-morphing network of DIY collectives and artist-run venues. Here, **public heritage meets punk ethos**, and high art intersects with activism, community engagement, and urban grit.

7.5.2 The Glasgow School of Art: Cradle of Creativity

At the heart of Glasgow's artistic legacy is the **Glasgow School of Art (GSA)**, both as a physical structure and as a cultural institution. Founded in 1845, the GSA has long been a beacon of artistic excellence, radical education, and innovation in design and fine art. Its alumni include **Charles Rennie Mackintosh**, **Douglas Gordon**, **Jenny Saville**, **David Shrigley**, and **Martin Boyce**—many of whom have gone on to shape the global art world.

Mackintosh's iconic 1909 GSA building—though tragically damaged by two major fires in 2014 and 2018—remains an enduring symbol of Glaswegian creativity. It represents not just architecture, but an ethos: one that values craftsmanship, originality, and the interconnection of art and daily life. Though restoration plans remain ongoing and controversial, the legacy of the GSA continues to animate the city's identity and artistic output.

The art school's influence spills out beyond its walls. Its annual degree show is a major cultural event, and its graduates often stay in Glasgow, seeding new collectives, exhibition spaces, and dialogues.

7.5.3 The Big Institutions: Kelvingrove, GoMA, and Riverside

While Glasgow prizes its independent spirit, it also boasts **major cultural institutions** that are impressive both in scale and ambition. These museums are not stagnant repositories of elite culture but are actively engaged in **rethinking colonial legacies, promoting inclusivity, and showcasing underrepresented voices**.

- **Kelvingrove Art Gallery and Museum**, opened in 1901, is one of Scotland's most visited attractions. Its grandeur lies not just in its Edwardian Baroque architecture but in its **juxtaposition of fine art and social history**. Paintings by Van Gogh and Salvador Dalí are displayed alongside natural history exhibits and artifacts from around the world. In recent years, Kelvingrove has taken strides to confront its colonial-era acquisitions, opening dialogues about repatriation and decolonization.

- **The Gallery of Modern Art (GoMA)**, housed in a neoclassical building in Royal Exchange Square, presents cutting-edge contemporary art in an accessible and central location. Its rotating exhibitions grapple with themes of **gender, race, social justice, and urban life**. The equestrian statue of the Duke of Wellington outside—perpetually topped with a traffic cone—has become a beloved symbol of the city's irreverent spirit, even as the institution inside works to dismantle the very hierarchies the Duke represents.

- **Riverside Museum**, designed by Zaha Hadid, is a gleaming monument to Glasgow's industrial past and maritime legacy. Its exhibits explore shipbuilding, transport, and working-class life with immersive, family-friendly displays. Yet beneath the nostalgia is a clear message: **Glasgow's transformation is as much about remembering as it is about reimagining**.

7.5.4 The Burrell Collection and Pollok Park: Art in the Landscape

In the tranquil setting of **Pollok Country Park**, the **Burrell Collection** houses a remarkable array of over 9,000 objects, donated to the city by shipping magnate Sir William Burrell. Recently refurbished with a focus on sustainability and accessibility, the museum combines medieval stained glass, Chinese ceramics, Impressionist paintings, and Islamic art into a deeply contemplative space.

Unlike many traditional collections, the Burrell is uniquely embedded in nature. Floor-to-ceiling glass walls allow the forest outside to permeate the viewing experience, suggesting that **art need not be separated from the living world.**

7.5.5 Beyond the Frame: Glasgow International and Biennial Energy

The **Glasgow International Festival of Contemporary Art**, held every two years, is a platform where **institutional and grassroots practices collide**. The festival brings together large-scale installations at major venues with experimental shows in forgotten basements, railway arches, and temporary studios.

Themes range from decolonial futurism to climate grief, from queer utopias to post-industrial landscapes. The festival is not only a showcase but a **snapshot of the city's shifting cultural currents**—a map of its tensions and transformations.

Past participants have included Turner Prize winners, street artists, and emerging local collectives. Importantly, the festival often takes place **outside the gallery walls**, reclaiming urban space as a site of dialogue and disruption.

7.5.6 DIY Culture and Artist-Run Spaces: The Soul of the Scene

If the big institutions provide prestige and public access, the **DIY and artist-run scene** provides freedom, experimentation, and radical possibility. Glasgow's visual arts reputation is inseparable from these smaller, often precariously funded spaces that operate out of sheer determination and communal effort.

- **Transmission Gallery**, founded in 1983, has become an institution in its own right. Run by and for artists, Transmission prioritizes **emerging practices, experimental media, and political engagement**. It has launched countless careers and remains a fiercely independent voice.

- **The Pipe Factory** and **David Dale Gallery**, located in former industrial buildings, provide platforms for contemporary exhibitions, residencies, and performances that interrogate the urban environment and art's role in public life.

- **SWG3**, while also a music and event space, hosts **exhibitions, mural projects, and studio spaces** that bridge visual art with design, fashion, and performance. Its walls are canvases, its venues are fluid, and its atmosphere is part punk, part progressive.

- **Civic House**, part of a growing network of socially engaged venues, merges co-working with cultural programming. It reflects a newer ethos of sustainability, cross-disciplinary practice, and community-rooted creativity.

Many of these spaces exist on the margins of funding and visibility, but it is precisely there that **some of the most vital, urgent work takes place**. These are not places of commercial gain, but of communal articulation—where identities are forged and futures imagined.

7.5.7 Art as Resistance: Murals, Activism, and the Everyday

Glasgow's **street art and mural scene**—already covered in 7.3—also reflects a broader ethos: that **art is not just for galleries, but for the people**. Community murals in Govan, anti-racist banners in Govanhill, climate-themed installations on the Clyde—all speak to a city where art is inseparable from activism.

During events like COP26, artists took to the streets with wheatpaste posters, banners, and pop-up exhibitions that challenged the very premise of corporate environmentalism. Art collectives like **The Project Room** and **RaDICAL Futures** have used visual art as a means of protest, storytelling, and solidarity.

Glasgow's cultural institutions themselves have not been immune to critique. Protests around fossil fuel sponsorships, demands for greater representation of BIPOC and disabled artists, and calls for the decolonization of museum holdings reflect a **healthy tension between celebration and accountability**.

7.5.8 Accessibility, Equity, and the Future of Cultural Space

While Glasgow has made strides in opening its cultural doors, significant **barriers still remain**—economic, physical, racial, linguistic, and psychological.

- Access to arts education and gallery representation still tilts toward the privileged.
- Funding cuts and gentrification threaten DIY spaces and studio affordability.
- Physical access remains an issue in many historic venues, despite commitments to inclusion.

In response, a new generation of artists and curators are **rethinking what cultural accessibility looks like**—offering audio descriptions, sensory programming, multilingual signage, and partnerships with communities long excluded from the city's visual narrative.

Projects like **Artlink Central, Glasgow Disability Alliance's Culture Collective, and Govanhill Baths' People's Bank of Creativity** reflect an emergent vision of cultural democracy: one where **everyone, regardless of background, can see themselves in the story the city tells**.

7.5.9 Conclusion: A Living, Shifting Canvas

Glasgow's art scene is not static—it is alive, restless, and **unapologetically plural**. From the hallowed halls of Kelvingrove to a shipping container on the Clyde, from Turner Prize retrospectives to a student zine fair in Maryhill, the city continues to **curate itself in public**.

Art here is not just framed—it's argued over, defended, remade. It serves as both mirror and hammer, reflecting what Glasgow has been and chiseling what it might become.

In a city shaped by deindustrialization, migration, protest, and play, visual culture is not a luxury. It is a **necessity—a means of survival, expression, and collective imagination**. And the curators? They are everyone: artist, activist, neighbour, child, critic, walker-by.

Glasgow, in short, remains **a city that knows how to look—and how to be seen**.

Printed in Dunstable, United Kingdom